AF867732

AI VISUAL REFERENCE SERIES

AI in Change Management Visual Reference

Darian Batra

About This Series

Published by AI Awareness Limited, creators of the AI Awareness training programme (aiawareness.ai). This series distills the frameworks used in our enterprise training into a fast, visual, look-it-up format. It's written under a shared series name so that each volume can draw on whichever of our specialists knows that domain best — the same approach used by long-running reference series where consistency of format matters more than a single author's voice.

This is the second title in a growing series, each volume applying the same visual, look-it-up approach to a different professional domain. Titles currently in development include:

- AI in Cybersecurity Visual Reference
- AI in Human Resources Visual Reference
- AI in Financial Institutions Visual Reference
- AI in Healthcare Visual Reference

New titles are added regularly. Search "AI Awareness Visual Reference" or visit **www.aiawareness.ai** for the complete, up-to-date list.

Contents

How to Use This Book

This is not a book meant to be read start to finish in one sitting, and it will not ask you to.

Most business books are written as a single argument: one idea building on the last, chapter by chapter, until you reach a conclusion at the end. This book works differently. Every page stands on its own. Each one takes a single concept, a single question, or a single practical scenario, and gives you what you need to understand it, without requiring you to have read what came before.

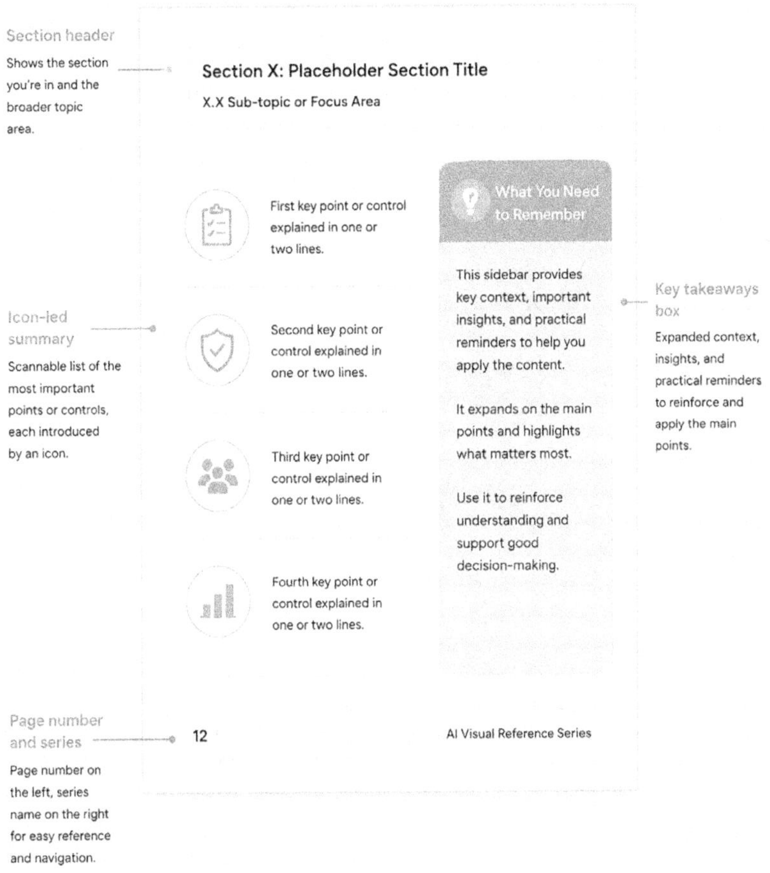

That means you should feel free to jump around. If a section title or a page heading catches your eye, open straight to it. If you are preparing for a specific meeting, facing a specific decision, or simply want a fast answer to a specific question, look it up directly rather than searching for it inside a longer chapter.

The table of contents is built to support this: it is organised by topic, not by a storyline you need to follow in order.

A few conventions repeat throughout the book, so a quick note on what to expect:

- Each section opens with a short page describing what it covers, so you can decide quickly whether it is the one you need.
- Most pages pair a visual, such as a diagram, a checklist, or an icon-led summary, with the practical explanation next to it.
- The visual is there to make the idea easier to scan and easier to recall later, not as decoration.
- Look for the "What You Need to Remember" box on many pages. It distils that page down to the two or three points most worth carrying with you, if that is all the time you have.

Keep this book somewhere you will reach for it again: on a desk, not a shelf. It is designed to be opened dozens of times, for a minute or two at a time, rather than once, cover to cover.

Introduction

Welcome to the AI Awareness: Visual Reference series.

Each book in this series takes a single professional domain and distills it into a format built for how people actually use reference material: not read once and shelved, but opened, scanned, and returned to. Every page pairs a clear visual with the essential point it supports, so a concept that might take three paragraphs to explain in a traditional guide can be grasped in seconds, and located again just as quickly the next time you need it. Book 1 in the series introduced this visual approach to AI awareness; this second volume applies it specifically to change management.

Change management has always been about people as much as process, and artificial intelligence is now reshaping both. AI can accelerate stakeholder analysis, communications, readiness assessments, and the countless documents a change programme generates, while the arrival of AI itself has become one of the largest changes most organisations are trying to manage.

What has shifted is the nature of the tools. Change leaders no longer work with a single, predictable system but with chatbots, copilots, and agents that draft, analyse, and increasingly act across the platforms a programme relies on. Playbooks built for a slower, more manual era do not take full advantage of this, nor do they address the new questions AI raises.

This volume sets out an AI-native approach to change management. It begins with foundations, then covers the tools and techniques change leaders can use, before applying AI across the full change lifecycle from early diagnosis to embedding and sustainment. It moves into functional and sector use cases, the governance, risk, and responsible adoption that keep AI use sound, and the organisational capability needed to keep pace as the tools evolve.

The focus is practical and specific rather than abstract. Each page pairs a clear visual with the essential point behind it, so an idea can be grasped in seconds and found again just as quickly when a programme is under pressure.

No technical background is required. Change touches every part of an organisation, and the ideas that matter most are the ones that hold up when explained plainly and shown clearly.

Wherever you sit in your organisation's change effort, we hope this book earns a place on your desk, not your shelf.

SECTION 1

AI-Native Change Management Foundations

This opening section reframes change management for an era in which AI is becoming embedded in everyday work. It begins with the new context for change leaders, asking why the discipline is being redefined, how organisations move from experimentation to embedded AI, what the shift from assistance to automation to agency means, and how the change leader's role is evolving.

It then grounds readers in the core AI concepts that matter in practice, covering generative AI for business work, predictive and analytical AI in change settings, agents and tool use, and the APIs, connectors, and integration that let AI join up with existing systems.

The section surveys today's product landscape, including ChatGPT for knowledge work and agentic execution, Claude for reasoning and document work, and Microsoft 365 Copilot across Word, Excel, and PowerPoint, with guidance on selecting the right platform mix.

Its largest part is human-centred change in an AI environment, addressing resistance, fear, and fatigue at scale, trust and transparency, designing for explainability, where humans stay accountable, and augmentation before replacement, including how to avoid the deskilling trap.

The section closes by treating adoption as a behavioural system shaped by habits, cues, incentives, and workflow integration. The aim is to give change professionals both the conceptual grounding and the human insight they need before applying specific tools. By the end you should understand how AI changes the practice of change management itself, not just the projects change teams are asked to support.

Why Change Management Is Being Redefined

How AI Is Changing the Pace of Change

1. **Timelines compress**
   Initiatives expected in weeks, not quarters.
2. **Decisions go data-first**
   Leaders lean on AI analysis, not just intuition.
3. **Automation climbs the skills ladder**
   Drafting, analysis, and synthesis become partially automated.
4. **Old frameworks strain**
   Linear, stage-based models struggle with continuous releases.
5. **Rules of the game shift**
   New tensions around who decides, who is accountable.

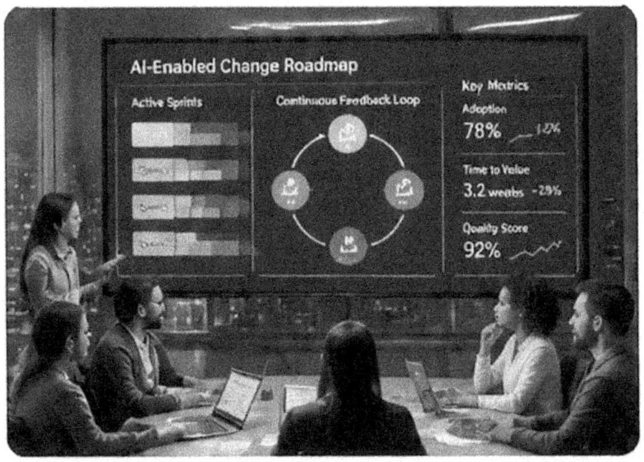

What you Need to Remember

Redesign for speed, not chaos.
Shorten planning cycles,
keep feedback loops always on.

Keep humans in charge of judgement.
Use AI to surface options;
people still own the calls and the risk.

Treat adoption as ongoing, not done.
Support people through rolling
releases and evolving tools.

From Linear Change to Living Change

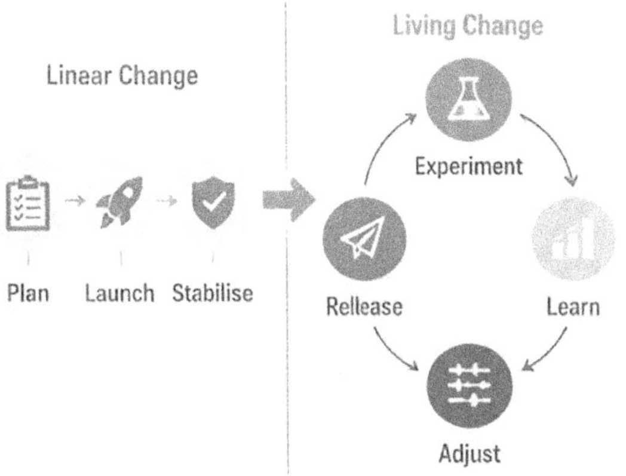

Shift governance, comms, and training
to match a continuous cycle.

Questions to ask

- Where will AI compress our timelines most?
- What assumptions in our current framework break?

Watch-outs

- Shadow decisions made only by tools
- People overwhelmed by constant tweaks.

Next steps

- Pilot one AI-enabled change using a faster cycle
- Document who is accountable at each decision point.

From Experimentation to Embedded AI

Shifting from Pilots to Everyday AI

1. **Pilots are over**
   Move from isolated experiments to real work and real outcomes.
2. **AI lives in everyday tools**
   People use AI where they already work.
3. **Change is persistent, not project-based**
   This is a never-ending cycle, not a one-time rollout.
4. **Adoption = ongoing behaviour shift**
   Small steps compound into lasting change.
5. **Leaders manage a moving target**
   Continuously adjust priorities, resources, and expectations.

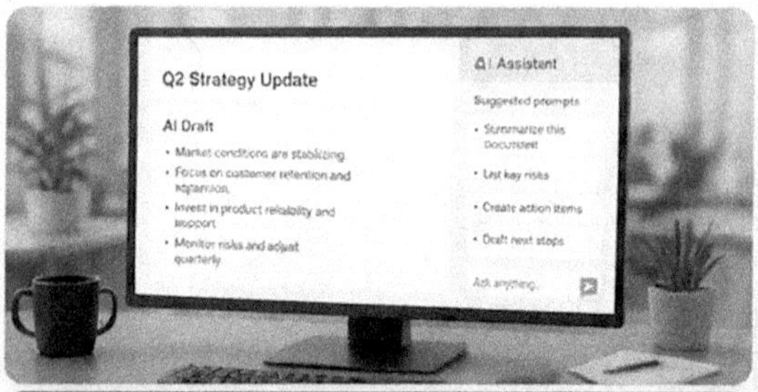

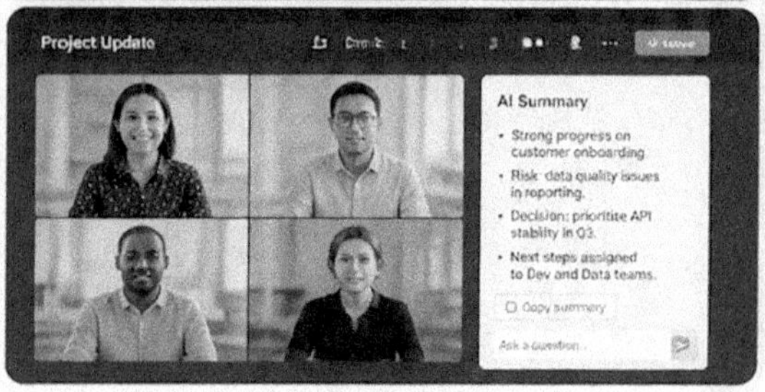

What you Need to Remember

AI is now part of the workplace fabric

It's embedded in tools, teams, and decisions every day.

You can't 'finish' this change

It evolves as the technology, people, and risks evolve.

Design for continuous learning and guardrails

Enable safe experimentation, iterate fast, and stay protected.

Update → **Experiment** → **Embed** → **Support**

- **Update**: Stay informed and adapt policies.
- **Experiment**: Try, test, and learn with real work.
- **Embed**: Make it part of tools and workflows.
- **Support**: Provide help, monitor, and improve.

Questions to Ask

- Where does AI already show up?
- Where must our behaviour change?
- How will we measure impact?

Signals You're Adapting

- People are seeking AI help.
- Workflows are being updated.
- Policies and guardrails evolve.

Next Step

Replace 'train and go live' with continuous enablement.

Assistance, Automation, and Agency

Three Modes of AI Work

1

Copilots Assist

- Respond when you ask
- Enhance the work you're already doing
- Human stays in the loop at every step

2

Automated Workflows

- Run on triggers or schedules
- No human needed to start each run
- Great for repeatable tasks like reports and intake

3

Agents Act

- Plan multi-step work
- Use tools and search for information
- Can complete tasks end-to-end

What you Need to Remember

Different modes, different implications.

Copilots, workflows, and agents change people's work in different ways. Be explicit about which you're using and why.

Keep humans accountable.

Ensure it's always clear who is responsible for outcomes, especially as autonomy increases in agent mode.

Design change by mode.

Tailor stakeholder conversations, controls, and training to the level of automation, from assistive to fully delegated.

Match the mode to the work, not the hype.

Assist	Automate	Delegate
Human leads, AI suggests.	AI runs the routine.	AI executes, human oversees.

Questions for Change Leaders

- ☐ What mode fits this problem best?
- ☐ Where must a human stay in the loop?
- ☐ What guardrails and monitoring are required?

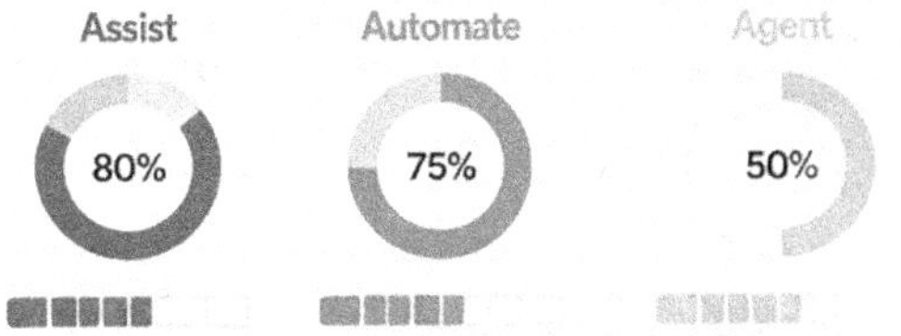

Increase autonomy gradually as governance matures.

The Evolving Role of the Change Leader

From Classic Change Manager to Transformation Orchestrator

1. **Classic toolkit**
   Stakeholders, comms, training, resistance management.
2. **Work is being rewired**
   AI reshapes tasks, decisions, and who does what.
3. **Go deeper into the workflow**
   Join conversations on tool design, data, and governance.
4. **Orchestrate people, process, and AI**
   Connect decisions, handoffs, and feedback loops.
5. **Human judgement stays at the centre**
   Guardrails, escalation paths, and values come from people.

What you Need to Remember

Think beyond communications
Shape how work is structured, not just how it is announced.

Sit at the design table
Partner with IT, ops, and product to influence tools and workflows.

Be the transformation orchestrator
Align people, process, and AI so the change actually lands.

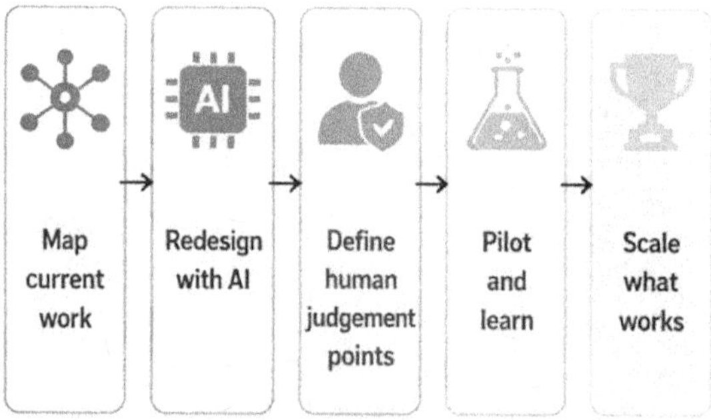

Questions to Ask in Every AI Change

- Where does AI change who decides what?
- What new skills do people need?
- How will we spot when the design isn't working?

Signals You're Playing the New Role Well

- You're invited early to AI and workflow design discussions.
- Leaders ask you about orchestration, not just comms.
- Teams say the new way of working feels clearer and more coherent.

Topic Introduction: Core AI Concepts That Matter in Practice

Your Practical Mental Model of AI

1. **Generative AI =** **creates new content** (text, images, code).

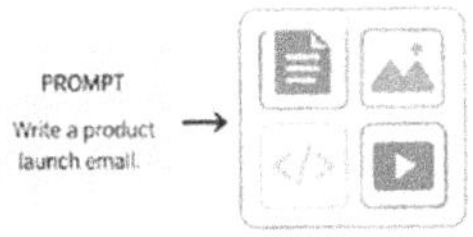

2. **Predictive & analytical AI =** scores, forecasts, detects patterns.

3. **Agents & tool use =** AI that can act, not just chat.

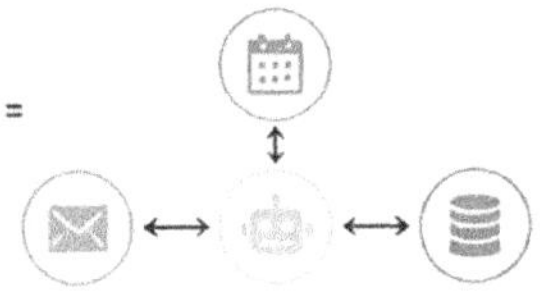

4. **Workflow integration =** AI plugged into existing systems.

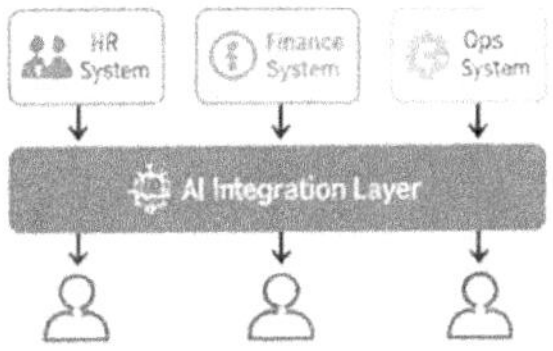

What you Need to Remember

Focus on understanding behaviour, not the maths.
The goal is better decisions, not complex formulas.

Use the four concepts to frame every AI conversation.
They give you a simple, shared language across the business.

Your job is to ask sharp questions and set boundaries.
Good questions lead to safe, valuable AI outcomes.

Questions to Ask in Any AI Project

What value will this create?
Who benefits and how will success be measured?

What are the key risks?
What could go wrong and how will we control it?

What data is needed?
Do we have the right data, and is it trustworthy and compliant?

How does this fit our workflow?
Where will AI sit, and how will people work with it?

Footer: Putting Your Mental Model to Work

- Map where generative vs predictive AI fits today.
- Spot where agents could remove hand-offs.
- Mark workflows that need stronger human oversight.

Generative AI for Business Work

How Generative AI Helps Your Work

1. **Creates new content**
   Drafts emails, summaries, analyses, and structured outputs from your inputs.
2. **Accelerates core tasks**
   Drafting, summarising, analysing, and synthesising information across change artefacts.
3. **Input quality drives output**
   Clear context, instructions, and examples lead to sharper responses.
4. **Probabilistic, not 'the truth'**
   Models generate plausible text, not verified facts – always sense-check.
5. **Human + AI = best results**
   You stay accountable for judgement, tone, and final sign-off.

What you Need to Remember

Think in tasks, not tools.
Start with the work: 'draft a briefing, summarise this pack, analyse comments' – then choose the AI that helps.

Prompt like a briefing.
Give background, goal, audience, tone, and format. Ask for options, not perfection on the first try.

Review, refine, reuse.
Check outputs for accuracy and bias, edit them, then save good prompts and examples for next time.

1. **Provide context** – Share the background, goal, and what you need.
2. **Ask for a draft** – Give clear instructions and specify the format.
3. **Review & edit** – Check for accuracy, clarity, and bias. Edit it.
4. **Share or reuse** – Share the final output or save the prompt to reuse later.

Good starting prompts
Purpose, audience, tone, format, deadline.

When NOT to rely on AI alone
High-risk decisions, legal wording, personal or sensitive data.

Build team habits
Share best prompts, create examples, and agree review steps.

Generative AI in Action — What It Looks Like

Four ways AI does the heavy lifting

1. **Drafting**
   AI creates a first draft in seconds.
2. **Summarising**
   AI condenses long content into key points.
3. **Analysing**
   AI finds patterns, insights, and anomalies.
4. **Synthesising**
   AI combines ideas and sources into new, coherent outputs.

What you Need to Remember

Think in workflows, not magic

AI excels at tasks in a process. Map the workflow, define inputs and outputs, and let AI handle the middle.

Ask for structure, not just answers

Clear instructions, formats, and examples lead to better, more usable results.

Keep humans on judgement

AI can inform your decisions, but only humans own context, values, and accountability.

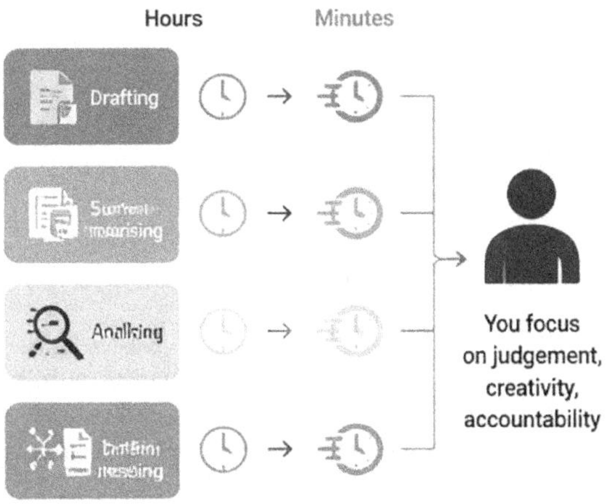

Where to try this next

Start with real work documents:

- Project plans and proposals

Good prompts to start with

- "Summarise this document into 5 key points."

Watch out for

- Over-trust in AI outputs
- Missing important context

Predictive and Analytical AI in Change Settings

Using Predictive & Analytical AI in Change

1 Spot patterns in existing data

Use historical data to forecast resistance, readiness risk, and adoption pace across teams and time.

2 Read signals across many sources

Combine surveys, usage logs, sentiment data, and operational signals—both structured and unstructured.

3 Intervene earlier, not after fires start

Act on leading indicators and risk signals to take proactive, evidence-based action before issues escalate.

4 Partner with data teams, don't code the models

Change leaders ask better questions, interpret insights, and know what's possible—leave the heavy lifting to experts.

What you Need to Remember

Predictive ≠ Generative

Predictive AI forecasts what may happen so we can act. Generative AI creates content. Different tools, different jobs.

Let data challenge gut feel

Data exposes blind spots and assumptions. Use it to test hypotheses and make fairer, more objective decisions.

Ask sharp questions of AI teams

The quality of insights depends on the quality of the questions, context, and business outcomes you define.

From data to action

1. Collect data →
2. Analyse & model →
3. Surface insights →
4. Target change actions

Better data → better insight → better change outcomes

Good questions to ask

- What outcome are we trying to predict?
- Which data do we trust most/least?
- How will we act on high-risk signals?

Warning signs

- Model outputs never change our plans
- We ignore data that contradicts leaders' views
- Nobody owns data quality

Where Predictive AI Shows Up in Change Work

Four Ways Predictive AI Supports Change

1 Readiness scoring
Combine surveys, role data, and training history to flag groups likely to struggle before go-live.

2 Resistance forecasting
Use sentiment from comments and pulse checks to spot emerging pushback early.

3 Adoption monitoring
Track real behaviours – logins, feature use, completion of key steps – not just training attendance.

4 Benefits realisation
Link adoption data to productivity, quality, or customer metrics so value is visible.

What you Need to Remember

Think risk and value.

Point models at where failure would really hurt or wins would really help.

Act before issues surface.

Treat predictions as early warning, then adjust comms, coaching, and support.

Humans still choose the response.

AI highlights patterns; change leaders decide what to do about them.

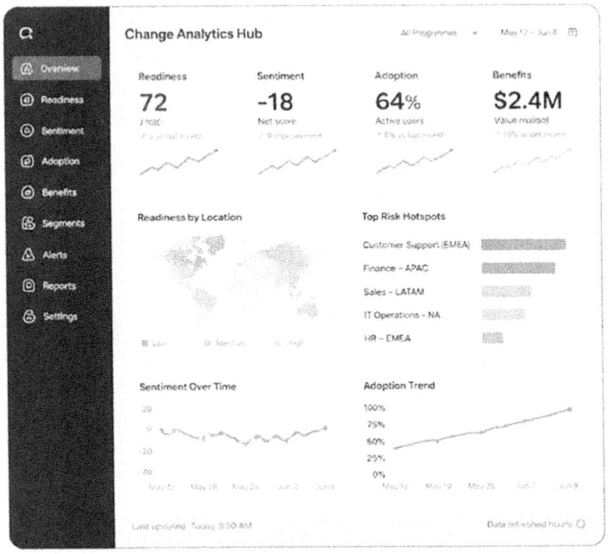

From Signals to Action

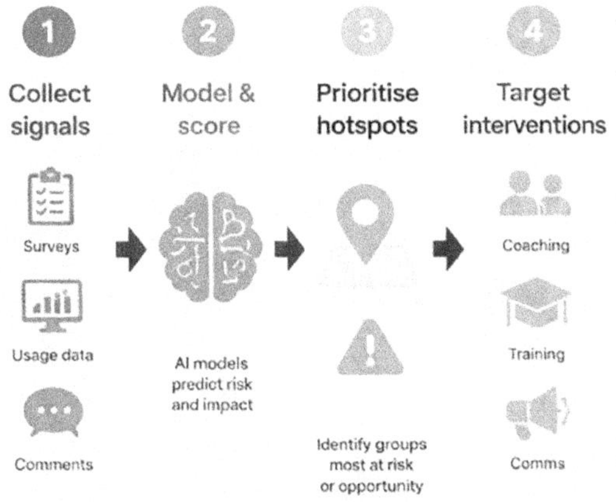

Right action • Right people • Right time

Good Ways to Use This in Your Programme

Start with one pilot area and a few clear metrics.

Share simple visuals with sponsors, not

Review predictions monthly and refine the questions

Agents and Tool Use

How agents work in practice

1. **Agent given a goal, plans multi-step tasks.**
   The agent breaks the goal into steps and creates a plan.

2. **Uses tools like web search, files, APIs, code.**
   The agent selects the right tool for each step.

3. **Passes outputs between steps autonomously.**
   Information flows between steps without human hand-offs.

4. **Levels of autonomy from guided copilot to fully delegated.**
   Choose the right level based on risk and complexity.

5. **Leaders design workflows and oversight.**
   Define guardrails, approvals, and monitoring.

What you Need to Remember

Think in goals, not prompts

Define the outcome you want.
Let the agent decide how to get there.

Match autonomy to risk

Use more autonomy for routine, low-risk work. Keep humans in the loop for high-impact decisions.

Leaders focus on design and governance

Design great workflows.
Set guardrails, monitor outcomes, and improve continuously.

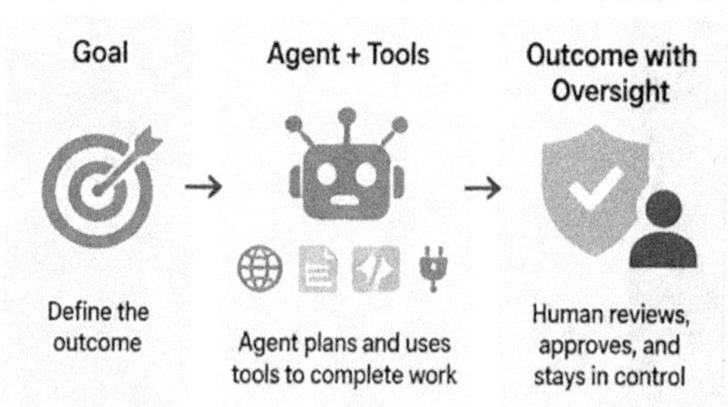

Quick checks for change leaders

- Are we clear on the goal and success criteria?
- Do we have the right tools and access in place?
- Are guardrails, monitoring, and reviews defined?

Define goals and success | Set guardrails and oversight | Design workflows that scale

What Makes an Agent Different from a Chatbot

From Reactive Chatbot to Goal-Driven Agent

1. Chatbots respond to one message at a time; agents plan across multiple steps to reach a goal.
2. Agents keep task memory: they track progress, learn from failures, and adjust their plan.
3. Agents can call tools and systems - search, calculate, update records, trigger workflows.
4. Agents can run on schedules or events, not just when a person types a prompt.
5. This shifts AI from "helpful assistant" to an active teammate in real workflows.

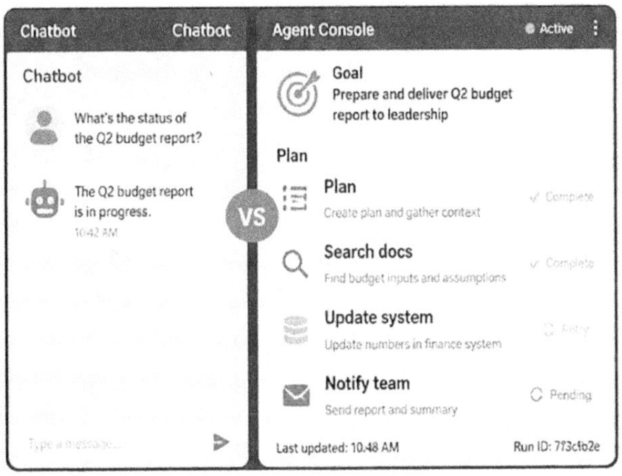

What you Need to Remember

Agents work toward goals, not just replies.

They plan multiple steps and use tools to achieve outcomes.

Agents keep context and can recover.

They remember across steps and try alternatives when something fails.

Agents can act without a human in the loop.

They can run on schedules or events. **Higher impact, higher risk—so they need clear guardrails and human checkpoints.**

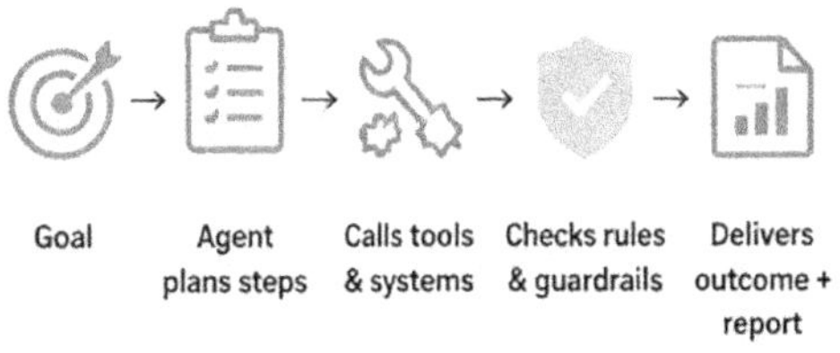

Define the goal and allowed tools for every agent.

Decide where humans must approve or review.

Monitor agents in production and refine rules.

APIs, Connectors, and Workflow Integration

How APIs and Connectors Work

1. **Connect systems**
   APIs act as secure plugs that let apps talk to each other.
2. **Exchange data**
   APIs send and receive data so systems stay in sync.
3. **Store and retrieve**
   Data is stored, organized, and retrieved when needed.
4. **Trigger actions**
   APIs or connectors start actions and automate next steps.
5. **Share outcomes**
   Results are shared back to the right people and places.

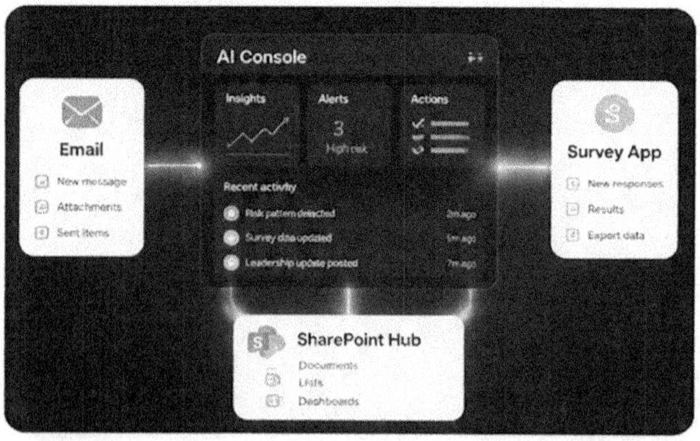

Example Workflow: Readiness Survey to Leadership Update

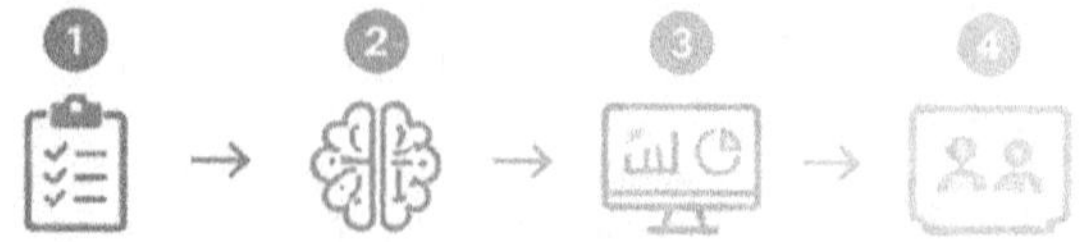

1. Survey responses captured
2. AI analyses risk patterns
3. Dashboard auto-updated
4. Summary posted to leaders' channel

What you Need to Remember

APIs embed AI into the flow of work

- APIs are the plumbing that lets systems exchange data and trigger actions.
- Good APIs keep information accurate, timely, and secure across your tools.

Connectors lower the barrier to integration

- Connectors and no-code tools (like Power Automate) make it easy to build flows between apps.
- They reduce custom work and speed up delivery.

Design integrated change workflows

- Change leaders should weave AI into programmes so updates, alerts, and actions happen automatically.
- Start small, prove value, and scale the most impactful flows.

Questions to explore

- Where could live data improve decisions?
- Which actions should AI trigger?
- What updates should be automated?

Good integration signals

- Less manual updating and fewer handoffs
- Leaders get timely insights
- Data is accurate and always up to date

Next experiment

Pick one workflow and sketch an API/connector-powered version.

Why Integration Matters for Change Leaders

Designing Integrated AI for Change

1. **Cut manual hopping between tools.**
   Integrate AI where people already work so insights appear in-flow, not in separate apps.
2. **Use real-time metrics.**
   Connect HR, project, and sentiment data so adoption and impact update continuously.
3. **Let AI surface weak signals.**
   Integrated AI flags pattern changes and risks without someone needing to 'go check'.
4. **Watch the blast radius.**
   Connected systems can spread bad data fast or cross permission boundaries.
5. **Shape the requirements.**
   As a change leader, specify what data, workflows, and guardrails are acceptable.

What you Need to Remember

Integration removes friction.
Embed AI in core tools so people don't copy-paste data or run separate reports.

Realtime signals change the conversation.
Use live metrics to spot adoption issues early and adjust comms, training, or process.

You are a gatekeeper, not a passenger.
Challenge integrations that over-reach, and insist on clear permissions, audit trails, and human override paths.

Map the flows → Decide what AI can do → Set guardrails & alerts

Iterate with IT, data, and security partners.

Before launch: confirm data sources, owners, and permissions for every integration.

During rollout: watch for surprises in who gains access to what.

Afterwards: track both productivity gains and new risks raised.

ChatGPT for Knowledge Work and Agentic Execution

Using ChatGPT for Knowledge Work

1. **Rapid research & synthesis** – scan sources, compare perspectives, and surface key themes quickly.
2. **Fast first drafts** – policies, emails, slide outlines, FAQs, talking points.
3. **Agentic execution** – let ChatGPT run web lookups, code, and file operations to complete multi-step tasks.
4. **Canvas for live iteration** – organise sections, track comments, and refine content with your team.
5. **Custom GPTs** – reusable assistants tuned to specific roles, playbooks, and data sets.

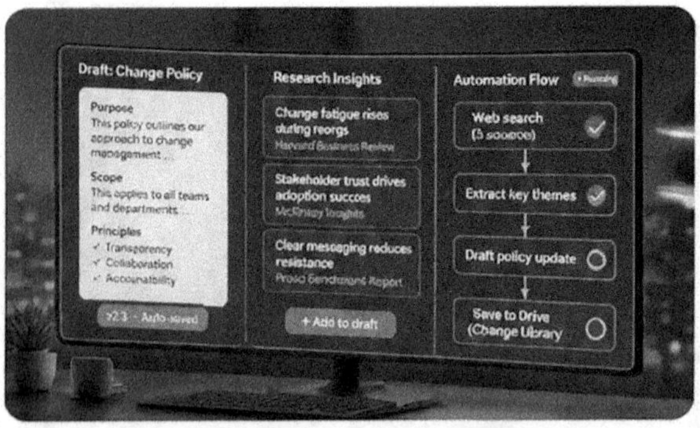

What you Need to Remember

Think 'co-worker', not chatbot.

Use ChatGPT to explore options, critique drafts, and co-design change artefacts – don't just ask for answers.

Aim for speed to first useful draft.

Get something on the page fast, then iterate with your own judgement and stakeholder input.

Let agents handle the busywork.

Automate research, formatting, and repetitive updates so humans focus on decisions and relationships.

From Prompt to Execution

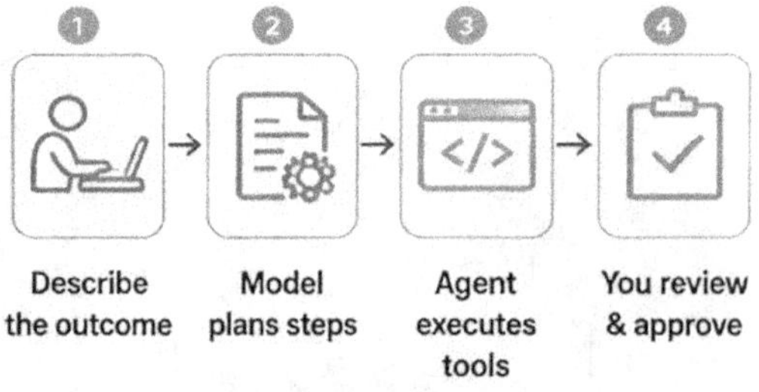

Good ways to start this week

- Pilot ChatGPT on one high-volume document type
- Create a simple custom GPT for your team
- Try a safe agent task: summarise and file meeting notes.

You're using it well when...

- You spend less time drafting and more time deciding
- Agent runs are transparent and easy to explain.

Claude for Reasoning, Document Work, and Structured Collaboration

When to Reach for Claude

1. **Careful reasoning and nuance**
   Use Claude when questions are ambiguous, sensitive, or need balanced judgement.

2. **Whole-doc thinking**
   Upload long reports, policy packs, or consultation responses and ask Claude to read across all of it.

3. **Structured analysis**
   Have Claude build outlines, tables, and frameworks that keep complex work organised.

4. **Governed workflows**
   Connect Claude to enterprise tools through skills and MCP-style integrations for controlled actions.

5. **High-stakes communication**
   Draft impact assessments, briefings, and stakeholder updates that need a stable, professional tone.

What you Need to Remember

Depth over speed.
Claude is at its best when you slow down the question and let it reason carefully.

Think in documents.
Work by giving Claude whole packs, then ask for structured summaries, comparisons, and risks.

Keep humans in charge.
Use skills and integrations to act on documents, but keep approvals and judgement with people.

Upload docs → Set goals & constraints → Claude analyses & drafts → You review, edit, and decide

Good prompts for Claude

- 'Read this whole pack and list the key decisions I need to make.'
- 'Compare these two policies and flag risks or gaps.'
- 'Turn this messy notes file into a clear briefing for executives.'

Guardrails to set

- State audience, tone, and red lines.
- Ask Claude to show reasoning, not just answers.
- Confirm anything sensitive with a colleague.

Microsoft 365 Copilot Across Word, Excel, and PowerPoint

How Copilot Works in Your Daily Apps

1 Word

- Draft change messages from a short brief.
- Tighten, rephrase, or adapt tone without leaving the file.

2 Excel

- Ask questions in natural language to explore data.
- Generate formulas, summaries, and charts automatically.

3 PowerPoint

- Build starter decks from prompts or documents.
- Refine structure, visuals, and speaker notes in seconds.

4 Copilot Agents

Chain tasks across apps, trigger workflows, and route updates—no coding skills needed.

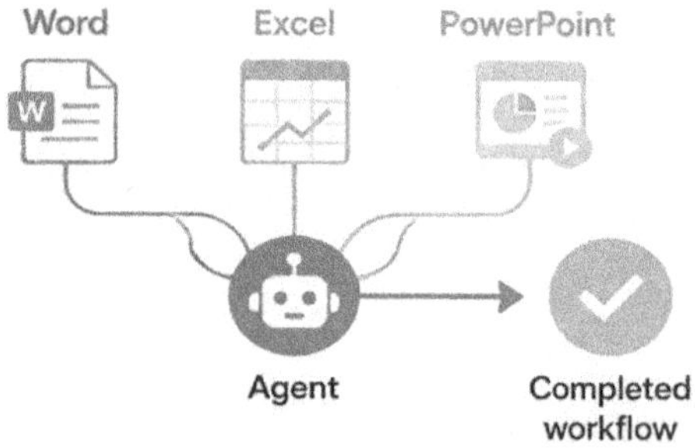

What you Need to Remember

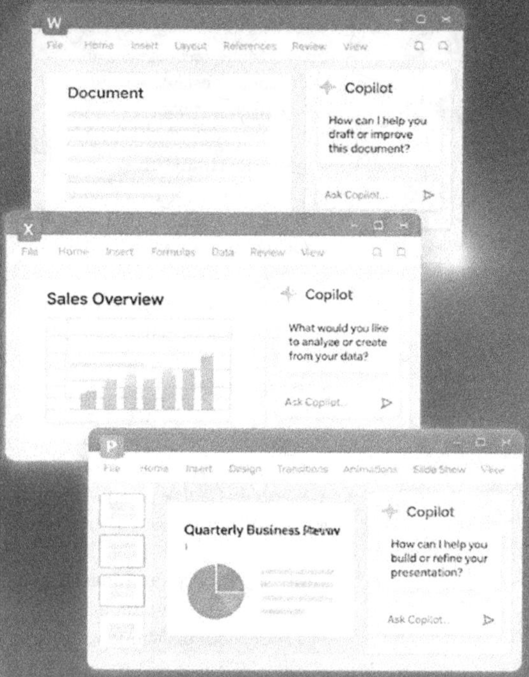

1. **Copilot lives where you already work.**
   No new app to learn—AI appears inside Word, Excel, and PowerPoint.
2. **You stay in control of the message and story.**
   Use Copilot for drafts, options, and analysis; you choose what is final.
3. **Start with high-impact use cases.**
   Target repetitive drafting, reporting, and slide creation to save the most time.

Good prompts

- State goal
- Share audience
- Paste context

When to use Copilot

- First drafts
- Data questions
- Slide clean-up

Checklist before sending

- Fact-check outputs
- Check tone and audience
- Remove sensitive data

Selecting the Right Platform Mix

Choosing by Task, Not Tool

1. **No single tool is best for every change task.**
   Match the platform to the work, not your preference.
2. **Use ChatGPT for speed and exploration.**
   Fast drafts, broad ideation, agent-style workflows on open tasks.
3. **Use Claude for depth and judgement.**
   Long documents, complex reasoning, and sensitive stakeholder messages.
4. **Use Microsoft 365 Copilot for enterprise delivery.**
   Slides, sheets, and docs that plug neatly into existing workflows.
5. **Run a light multi-tool model.**
   Blend tools across a project; switch as the task changes.

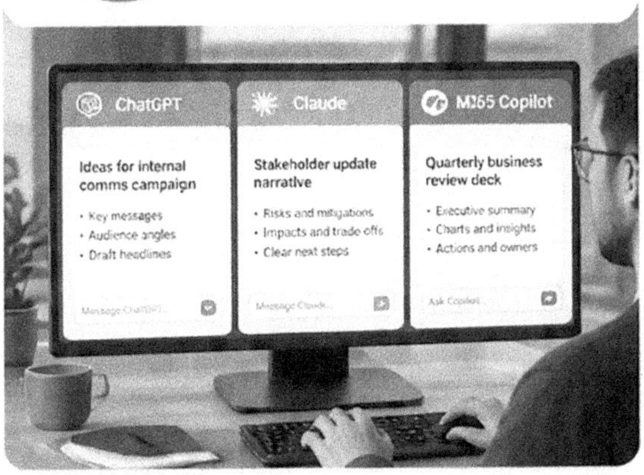

What you Need to Remember

Start from the task.
Clarify speed, depth, and format needs before you pick a tool.

Play to each platform's edge.
Use ChatGPT for rapid action, Claude for nuance, Copilot for polished artefacts.

Normalise switching tools.
Model tool-hopping so teams see it as smart practice, not inconsistency.

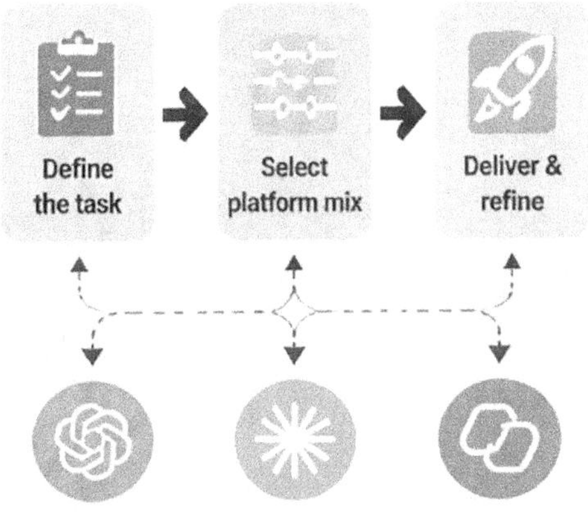

Mix and match the right tools for the task at hand.

Quick Checks

- Do I know the outcome I need?
- Have I picked the best tool

Risks to Watch

- Over-using one tool
- Unclear ownership

Next Experiment

Pick one change initiative and deliberately plan a

Human Resistance in the Age of AI

Four Faces of AI Resistance

1 Fear

Worry about job loss, status, and relevance.

2 Fatigue

Change overload after years of transformation.

3 Confusion

Unclear what AI does, how decisions are made, or who is in charge.

4 Role Uncertainty

Blurred boundary between human work and AI tasks.

What you Need to Remember

1. These reactions are rational, not 'difficult behaviour'.
2. Name the fears openly before selling benefits.
3. Design AI roles so humans stay in control of judgement and accountability.
4. Target early wins that reduce workload, not status.

Fear → Listen & acknowledge

Fatigue → Slow the pace & prioritise

Confusion → Explain how AI works & decide rules

Role Uncertainty → Clarify who does what

Questions to Ask Teams

- What worries you most about this AI?
- Which parts of your job feel 'at risk'?
- Where could AI remove drudgery?

Signals You're Making Progress

- People bring up AI concerns early
- Requests for training increase
- Staff suggest their own safe use cases

Design Principle

Protect human dignity, agency, and craft first; the tooling comes second.

Mapping the Fear and Fatigue Landscape

Role-based fear and fatigue map

1. **Operational roles – fear of task loss**
   Worry that automation will remove jobs or key tasks.

2. **Knowledge workers – deskilling and over-reliance**
   Concern that AI will weaken skills and critical thinking.

3. **Managers – accountability and control**
   Fear of losing oversight, authority, or team trust.

4. **Specialists – expertise commoditised**
   Anxiety that unique expertise will be replicated by AI.

5. **Why segment? – enables targeted responses**
   Understanding segments helps us address the right fears.

What you Need to Remember

Different roles, different stories

Fear and fatigue show up differently across roles.

Tailor AI conversations to each group's realities and pressures.

Name the fear, then normalise it

Acknowledge concerns openly.

When people feel seen, they're more open to change.

Design role-specific interventions

Adjust training, examples, and messaging to fit each role.

Provide role-relevant safeguards and clear escalation paths.

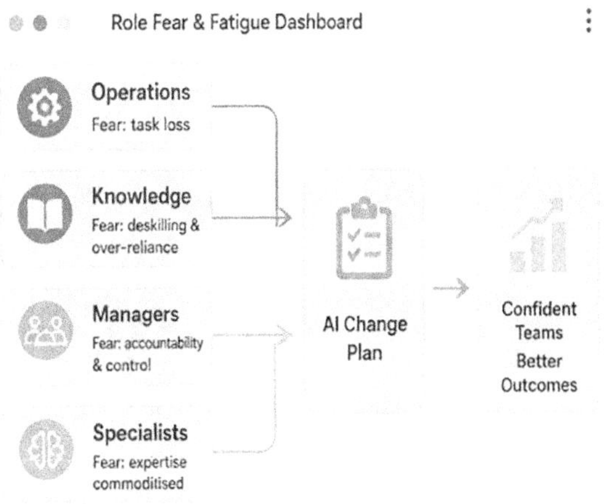

Questions to ask
What is each role most worried about losing or being judged for?

Signals of progress
People raise specific, not vague, concerns and ideas.

Next step
Draft one change action that directly addresses each role.

Practical Strategies for Resistance at Scale

Working with Resistance, Not Against It

1. **Acknowledge concerns out loud.**
   Name worries about AI instead of smoothing them over.
2. **Back early adopters as peers.**
   Let them share real stories, not scripted talking points.
3. **Create safe test zones.**
   Sandboxes and pilots where outcomes don't hit performance reviews.
4. **Draw the line.**
   Spell out what AI reshapes and what stays human-led.
5. **Chase small, visible wins.**
   Show concrete improvements before any big launch moment.

What you Need to Remember

- **Surface fears, don't suppress them.**
  People calm down when worries are seen, heard, and answered plainly.
- **Peers change minds faster than leaders.**
  Use respected colleagues to model honest, practical AI use.
- **Design the first wins on purpose.**
  Low-risk experiments plus clear boundaries turn anxiety into curiosity.

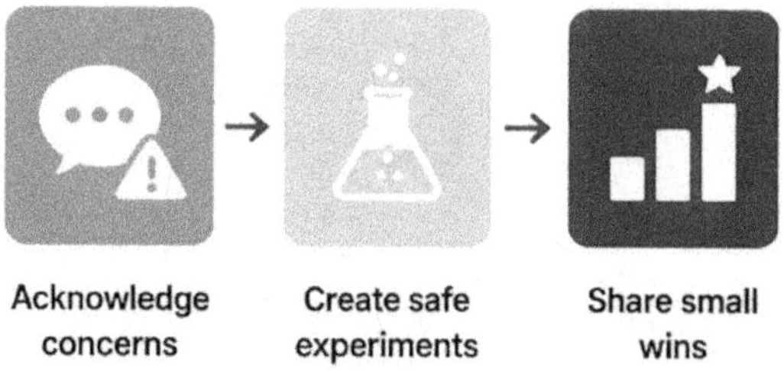

Questions to Guide Your Next Step

- Where is anxiety highest right now?
- Who are the most trusted early adopters?
- What's one safe AI experiment we can run this month?

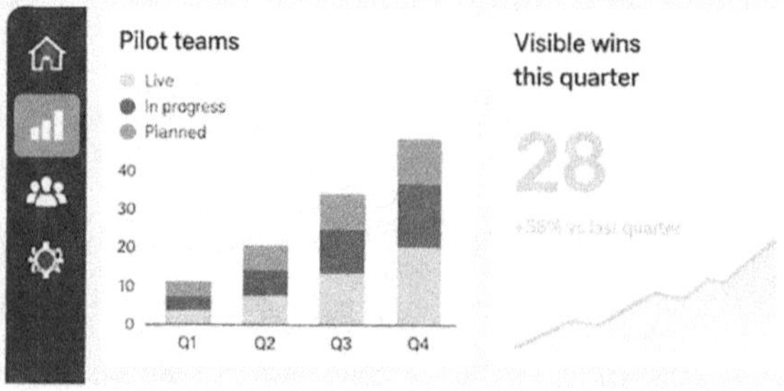

Trust and Transparency

Designing for Trust in AI

1. **Trust is designed, not assumed**
   Build trust into systems, processes, and experiences from the start.
2. **Explain how results were produced**
   Make reasoning, models, and data sources easy to understand.
3. **Show benefits AND limits**
   Be clear about what the AI can do well—and where it can't.
4. **Keep human accountability visible**
   Make it obvious who is responsible for reviews, approvals, and outcomes.
5. **Transparency creates psychological safety**
   Open systems build confidence and encourage people to speak up and share concerns.

What you Need to Remember

Make the AI explain itself

Share data sources, reasoning steps, and confidence – not just the final answer.

Be open about limits and errors

Set expectations, name what the AI might miss, and invite people to challenge outputs.

Keep a human clearly accountable

Show who reviewed or approved each AI-supported decision.

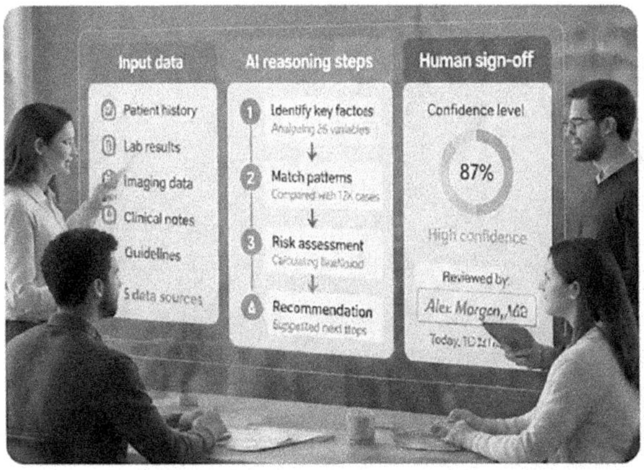

AI generates output → System explains why → Human reviews & decides → Decision recorded

Always show: data used, assumptions, reviewer.

Flag: low confidence, missing data, high impact decisions.

Invite feedback: "What doesn't make sense here?"

Designing for Explainability in Practice

Design Choices for Everyday Explainability

1. **Decide to be transparent.**
   Treat explainability as a core design requirement, not a 'nice-to-have' feature.
2. **Label AI outputs in the interface.**
   Tag summaries, recommendations, and drafted messages as 'AI-generated' wherever they appear.
3. **Build in human review.**
   Add a clear review step to every AI-assisted workflow so humans confirm or edit before anything is final.
4. **Show how the AI reached this.**
   Use short, plain-language reasons: key inputs, main factors, or rules behind the recommendation.
5. **Never ship a black box.**
   If people can't see or question the logic, don't deploy it—provide at least a brief rationale or example.

What you Need to Remember

Make AI visible.
Always label AI-generated content so people know when they're looking at machine output.

Keep humans in charge.
Position AI outputs as suggestions. Someone accountable reviews, edits, or rejects before action.

Explain, even briefly.
Give a one-sentence rationale or key factors for each important recommendation to build trust and confidence.

AI creates draft → Label + explain → Human reviews → Decision recorded

Design Checklist for Explainable Workflows

- Is every AI output clearly labelled?
- Where is human review documented?
- What explanation does each key recommendation show on screen?

Signals You've Got It Right

- People can point to where AI was used in a decision
- Reviewers feel confident challenging AI suggestions
- Issues are caught early because someone questioned the output.

Where Humans Stay Accountable

Keeping Accountability Human

1. **AI can inform, draft, and analyse — but humans own decisions.**
   AI provides input; humans take responsibility for outcomes.

2. **Define accountability boundaries before deployment.**
   Decide who is accountable, for what, and under which conditions.

3. **Identify decisions that must never be delegated to AI.**
   Includes performance, sensitive communication, and regulated risk decisions.

4. **Show when employees should override, escalate, or reject AI outputs.**
   Give people clear authority — and safe ways — to challenge AI.

5. **Clear accountability reduces anxiety and encourages responsible use.**
   People engage more when they know what they own.

What you Need to Remember

Make accountability explicit before tools launch.
Define roles, ownership, and escalation paths up front — not as an afterthought.

Protect non-delegable decisions.
Keep performance, sensitive communication, and regulated risk decisions firmly in human hands.

Expect and reward human overrides.
Build a culture where challenging AI is expected, respected, and recognized.

AI supports	Human judges	Human is accountable
AI provides data, insights, and recommendations.	Humans review context, apply judgement, and consider impacts.	Humans make the decision and own the outcome.

Questions to clarify

- Who owns this decision and why?
- What decisions must never be delegated to AI?
- When should people overrule or escalate AI?

Signals of healthy accountability

- Roles and responsibilities are clearly documented.
- People feel safe to challenge AI outputs.
- Overrides are tracked, reviewed, and learned from.

Watch-outs

- Blurred ownershiip of decisions.
- Non-delegable decisions slipped to AI.
- People afraid to overrule AI recommendations.

Augmentation Before Replacement

Leading with Augmentation

AI uplifts, not replaces

Start by using AI to remove friction so people can do their best work.

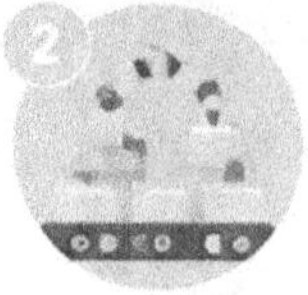

Let AI take the draining work

Automate repetitive, rules-based tasks and busywork.

Humans keep judgement and relationships

Protect work that needs experience, trust, and creativity.

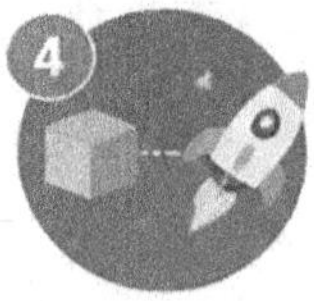

Frame AI as an upgrade

Talk about capability uplift, not cost-cutting or headcount.

Design early wins

Choose pilots that clearly help staff and prove the promise.

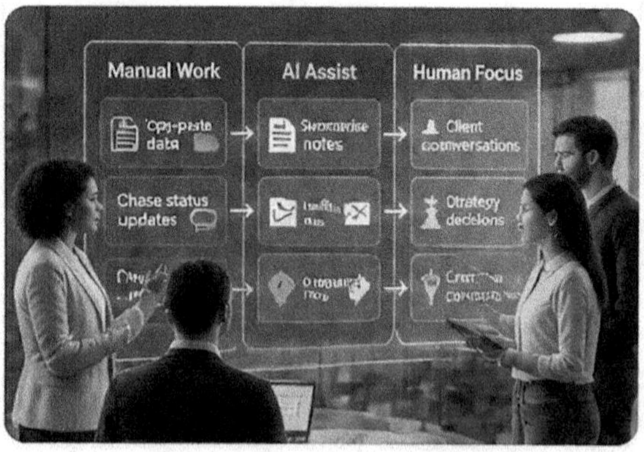

What you Need to Remember

Lead with the augmentation story.

Explain how AI removes the grind and makes people more capable.

Be honest, but focus on gains.

Acknowledge disruption, set expectations, and keep attention on better outcomes.

Shape first experiences so work feels better.

Pick visible, high-value use cases and celebrate early success.

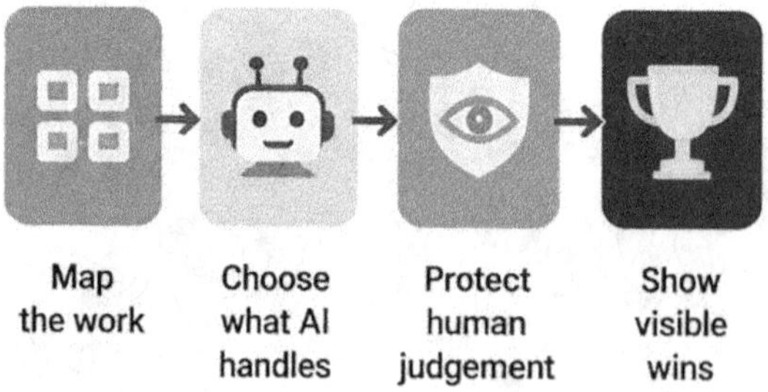

Good prompts for your team

- What parts of your job feel repetitive or draining?
- Where is human judgement critical?
- How will we know work is getting better?

Signals of successful augmentation

- People suggest their own AI use cases
- Complaints about busywork drop
- Teams ask for more AI support

Designing for Explainability in Practice

Design Choices for Everyday Explainability

1. **Decide to be transparent.**
Treat explainability as a core design requirement, not a 'nice-to-have' feature.

2. **Label AI outputs in the interface.**
Tag summaries, recommendations, and drafted messages as 'AI-generated' wherever they appear.

3. **Build in human review.**
Add a clear review step to every AI-assisted workflow so humans confirm or edit before anything is final.

4. **Show how the AI reached this.**
Use short, plain-language reasons: key inputs, main factors, or rules behind the recommendation.

5. **Never ship a black box.**
If people can't see or question the logic, don't deploy it—provide at least a brief rationale or example.

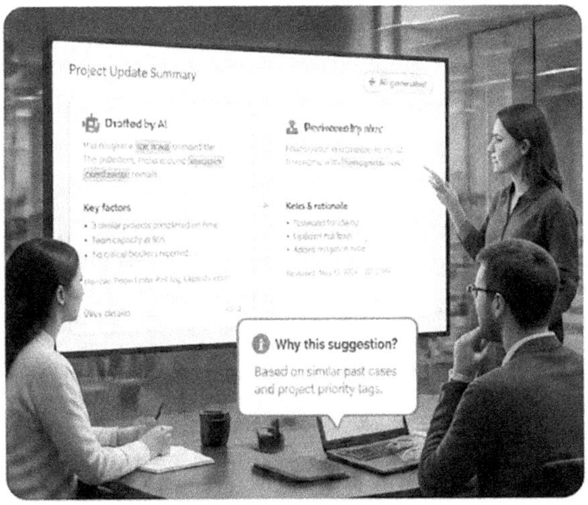

What you Need to Remember

Make AI visible.
Always label AI-generated content so people know when they're looking at machine output.

Keep humans in charge.
Position AI outputs as suggestions. Someone accountable reviews, edits, or rejects before action.

Explain, even briefly.
Give a one-sentence rationale or key factors for each important recommendation to build trust and confidence.

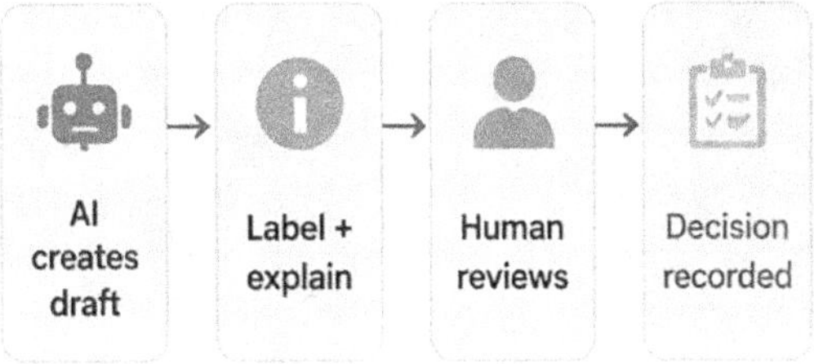

Design Checklist for Explainable Workflows

- Is every AI output clearly labelled?
- Where is human review documented?
- What explanation does each key recommendation show on screen?

Signals You've Got It Right

- People can point to where AI was used in a decision
- Reviewers feel confident challenging AI suggestions
- Issues are caught early because someone questioned the output.

Where Humans Stay Accountable

Keeping Accountability Human

1. **AI can inform, draft, and analyse — but humans own decisions.**
   AI provides input; humans take responsibility for outcomes.

2. **Define accountability boundaries before deployment.**
   Decide who is accountable, for what, and under which conditions.

3. **Identify decisions that must never be delegated to AI.**
   Includes performance, sensitive communication, and regulated risk decisions.

4. **Show when employees should override, escalate, or reject AI outputs.**
   Give people clear authority — and safe ways — to challenge AI.

5. **Clear accountability reduces anxiety and encourages responsible use.**
   People engage more when they know what they own.

What you Need to Remember

Make accountability explicit before tools launch.

Define roles, ownership, and escalation paths up front — not as an afterthought.

Protect non-delegable decisions.

Keep performance, sensitive communication, and regulated risk decisions firmly in human hands.

Expect and reward human overrides.

Build a culture where challenging AI is expected, respected, and recognized.

AI supports → **Human judges** → **Human is accountable**

- **AI supports**: AI provides data, insights, and recommendations.
- **Human judges**: Humans review context, apply judgement, and consider impacts.
- **Human is accountable**: Humans make the decision and own the outcome.

Questions to clarify

- Who owns this decision and why?
- What decisions must never be delegated to AI?
- When should people overrule or escalate AI?

Signals of healthy accountability

- Roles and responsibilities are clearly documented.
- People feel safe to challenge AI outputs.
- Overrides are tracked, reviewed, and learned from.

Watch-outs

- Blurred ownershiip of decisions.
- Non-delegable decisions slipped to AI.
- People afraid to overrule AI recommendations.

Augmentation Before Replacement

Leading with Augmentation

AI uplifts, not replaces
Start by using AI to remove friction so people can do their best work.

Let AI take the draining work
Automate repetitive, rules-based tasks and busywork.

Humans keep judgement and relationships
Protect work that needs experience, trust, and creativity.

Frame AI as an upgrade
Talk about capability uplift, not cost-cutting or headcount.

Design early wins
Choose pilots that clearly help staff and prove the promise.

What you Need to Remember

Lead with the augmentation story.

Explain how AI removes the grind and makes people more capable.

Be honest, but focus on gains.

Acknowledge disruption, set expectations, and keep attention on better outcomes.

Shape first experiences so work feels better.

Pick visible, high-value use cases and celebrate early success.

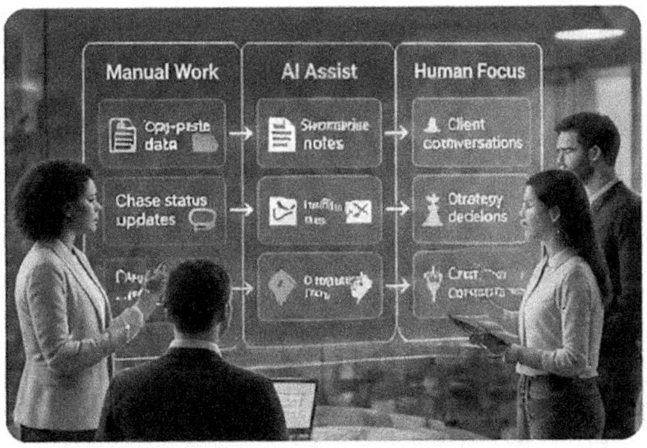

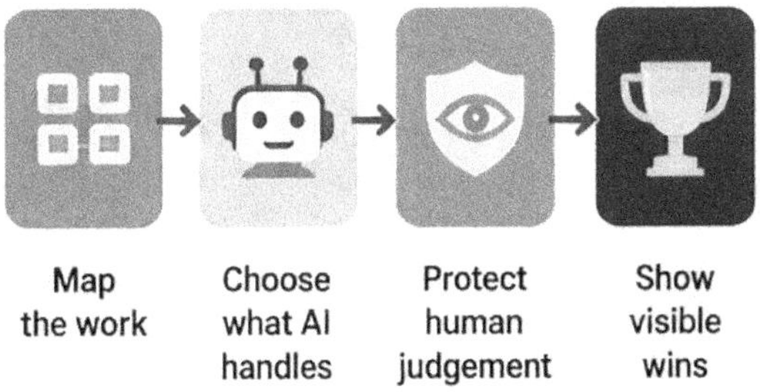

Good prompts for your team

- What parts of your job feel repetitive or draining?
- Where is human judgement critical?
- How will we know work is getting better?

Signals of successful augmentation

- People suggest their own AI use cases
- Complaints about busywork drop
- Teams ask for more AI support

Designing Uplift Into the Adoption Journey

Designing uplift into everyday work

1 Find the draining tasks.

- Identify repetitive, manual, low-value work.
- Listen to what people avoid or postpone.

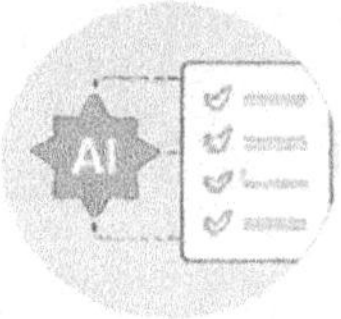

2 Map tasks to AI capability.

- Match the task to a specific AI tool or feature.
- Ensure the output is accurate, reliable, and easy to use.

3 Prioritise quick, visible wins.

- Start small where success is fast and measurable.
- Focus on outcomes people care about.

4 Use wins to build confidence.

- Celebrate results and share real stories.
- Reinforce that AI helps, people decide.

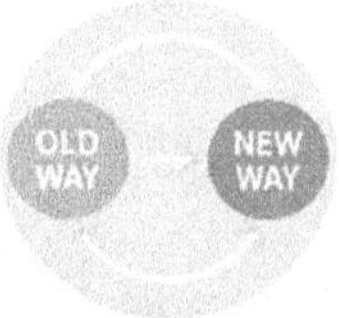

5 Let people feel the benefit before asking habit change.

- Experience the uplift first.
- Then guide the shift to the new way of working.

What you Need to Remember

Start from human pain, not AI features.

Understand the real work people find hard or draining. Solutions must solve their problems, not showcase technology.

Make early wins obvious and measurable.

Pick use cases with fast impact and clear metrics. Visibility builds belief and momentum.

Sequence the journey: feel the uplift, then shift the habit.

Let people experience the benefit first. Then guide the change with support, training, and clear expectations.

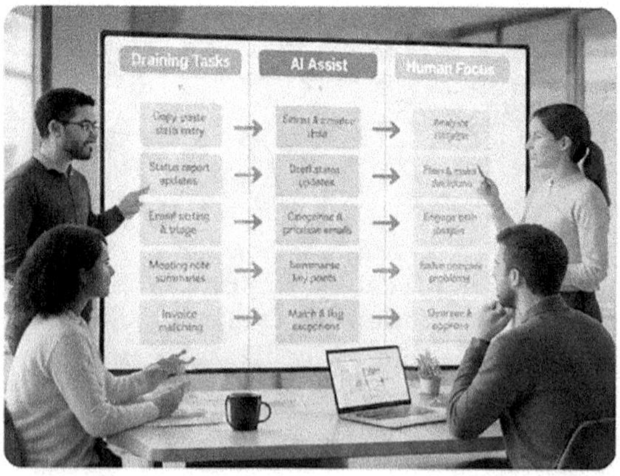

1. **Listen to roles** — Understand real work, pain points, and goals.
2. **Match AI to tasks** — Map the right AI capabilities to the work.
3. **Launch quick wins** — Deliver fast, measurable impact.
4. **Scale harder use cases** — Build on success and tackle more complex work.

Good prompts for discovery interviews

- What tasks drain your time or energy the most?
- Where do errors, rework, or delays happen?
- If you had a magic assistant, what would you want it to do for you?

Signals of real uplift

- Fewer complaints about busywork.
- People ask for more automation.
- Time saved is tracked and shared.

Avoiding the Deskilling Trap

1 Spot the risk
Over-reliance on AI quietly erodes skills people still need.

2 Protect core skills
Keep critical thinking, judgement, and expertise in regular use.

3 Interrogate the output
Ask: What's missing? What doesn't fit? What would I do differently?

4 Design mixed workflows
AI handles | You practise
Let AI draft and sort, but ensure humans still analyse, decide, and explain.

5 Raise the ceiling, not lower the floor
Use AI to extend capability, never as an excuse to accept weaker skills.

What you Need to Remember

Keep humans credible.
People must still be able to produce solid work without AI. Protect writing, analysis, and domain knowledge.

Make questioning normal.
Build a culture where checking, comparing sources, and pushing back on AI is expected, not optional.

Design for long-term skill health.
Choose workflows where AI speeds the grunt work, while humans still think, decide, and explain outcomes.

AI draft → Human critique → Revise together → Final human sign-off

Ask: If AI failed, could we still do this well?

Track: Is independent skill getting better, worse, or invisible?

Aim: AI that amplifies judgement, not replaces it.

SECTION 2

AI Tools and Techniques for Change Leaders

Here we look at the practical tools and techniques change leaders can put to work day to day. The section opens with prompting for change management, covering prompt structures that work, prompting for different change artefacts, iterative prompting and critique loops, and building prompt libraries and reusable templates. It then examines working with agents and agent mode, explaining what agent mode changes in practice, how to design safe agent tasks, how to supervise agents effectively, and when to reach for chat, Copilot, or an agent.

A substantial part is devoted to working with documents, data, and presentations, showing how to draft change narratives and revise policies in Word, produce stakeholder packs and targeted communications, run readiness analysis and sentiment trends and track benefits in Excel, and build executive decks and training slides in PowerPoint, before orchestrating these tools together across a set of change deliverables.

The final part turns to using APIs and automation in change programmes, considering when API-based workflows are worth the effort, simple workflow patterns, connecting AI to enterprise tools, and moving from prototype to production. The emphasis is on repeatable methods that fit the real artefacts change teams produce, rather than isolated clever prompts.

By the end you should be able to prompt with intent, delegate suitable tasks to agents under supervision, and assemble cross-tool workflows that speed up the documents, analysis, and communications at the heart of change work.

Prompt Structures that Work

5 BUILDING BLOCKS OF A STRONG PROMPT

1. **Context** — Give the background and key details.
2. **Task** — State exactly what you want done.
3. **Audience** — Make clear who it's for.
4. **Format** — Specify the structure or output style.
5. **Constraints** — Set limits, rules, or requirements.

WHAT YOU NEED TO REMEMBER

Structure first, wording second.

A clear structure helps the AI understand your intent and produce better results.

Always say who it's for.

The audience shapes tone, depth, examples, and level of detail.

Tell the AI how to package the answer.

Specify the format so the output is easy to use, scan, and act on.

1	2	3	4	5
Context	**Task**	**Audience**	**Format**	**Constraints**
Background and details	What you want done	Who it's for	How the answer should look	Rules and limits

QUICK PROMPT TEMPLATE

Context + Task + Audience + Format + Constraints

- Add details to each part.
- Keep it specific and clear.
- Refine based on results.

BEFORE YOU HIT ENTER, CHECK...

- Is the goal crystal clear?
- Did I name the audience?
- Is the format specified?

COMMON FAILURE MODES

- Vague or missing context.
- No audience specified.
- Unclear task or mixed goals.
- No format or constraints.

Prompting for Different Change Artefacts

Shaping prompts to match the artefact

1 Leadership briefings & summaries – explain to 'front-load context and decisions'

- Outline strategy and why it matters now
- Spell out the decision, options, and timelines
- Ask for: endorse, decide, or challenge

2 Stakeholder emails – focus on 'audience, tone, and action'

- Name the audience role and attitude
- Set tone: reassuring, urgent, exploratory
- End with 1–2 clear actions and deadlines

3 FAQs – prompts about 'real questions people ask'

- List top employee worries in natural language
- Ask for short, plain-English answers
- Group by theme: impact, timing, support

4 Plans – prompts that request structure

- Specify table with tasks, owners, dates, status
- Ask for milestones and dependencies
- Include change, comms, and training workstreams

5 Risk logs – structured risk thinking

- Request columns for risk, cause, impact, likelihood, owner, response
- Ask for early warning signals
- Include both people and delivery risks

6 Training content – designing for learning

- State learner level and prior knowledge
- Give a clear learning outcome
- Specify format: workshop, webinar, e-learning, job aid

What you Need to Remember

1. Start with the artefact
Prompts describe the deliverable first.

2. Name audience, purpose, and outcome
Who it's for and what decision or action it should drive.

3. Ask for structure when you need it
Tables, numbered steps, or fields.

4. Feed in real concerns and examples
Use actual questions, objections, and scenarios from your change.

AI Prompt Assistant

Briefing Create a leadership briefing that explains our change initiative, the decision needed, options, timelines, and risks. Ask leaders to decide by [date].

Email Write an email to [audience] about the change. Keep the tone [reassuring]. Explain what's changing, why it matters, and ask them to [action] by [date].

FAQ List the top questions employees will ask about this change. Provide short, plain-English answers grouped by impact, timing, and support.

Mini prompt checklist

- Artefact?
- Audience?
- Format?
- Decision or action?

Try this now

Rewrite one current change task as three prompts: briefing, email, FAQ.

Common failure mode

Vague prompts that ignore audience and format produce generic, unusable output.

Iterative Prompting and Critique Loops

Working with Iterative Prompts

1. **Treat first draft as a sketch.**
   Use the first output to get ideas on the page, not as the final.
2. **Ask the AI to critique its own work.**
   AI can spot weak spots you might miss.
3. **Give targeted feedback on tone, structure, length, accuracy.**
   Be specific so the next draft moves closer to your goal.
4. **Refine in layers, one aspect per pass.**
   Change one thing at a time to see clear improvement.
5. **Stop when it's good enough to use.**
   Perfect is impossible. Usable is the goal.

What you Need to Remember

Don't accept the first draft.
The first output is a starting point, not the finished product.
Better results come from iteration.

Direct the critique with specific asks.
Clear, targeted feedback leads to better revisions.
Vague prompts get vague results.

Aim for 'usable', not 'perfect'.
Perfection slows you down.
Usable is what creates impact.

Draft 1		Draft 3	
Tone	Formal	Tone	Conversational
Structure	Dense	Structure	Clear
Length	Long	Length	Concise
Clarity	Medium	Clarity	High

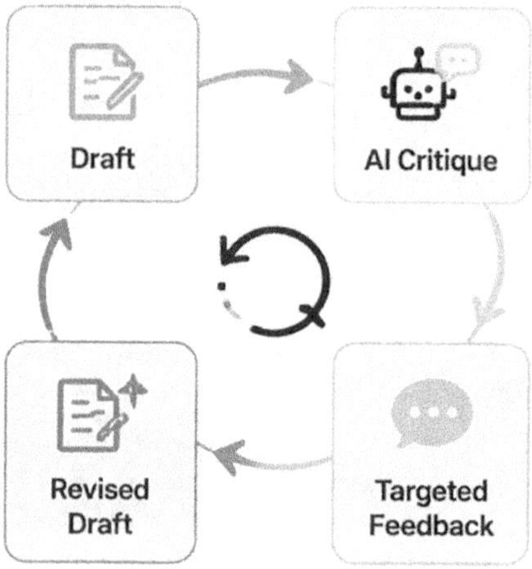

Fix tone, then structure, then length.

Tell the AI who the audience is.

STOP Stop iterating once the output does the job.

Prompt Libraries and Reusable Templates

Building a Prompt Library

1. **What a prompt library is**
   A central place to collect, organize, and reuse high-quality prompts.

2. **Saves time on repeat work**
   Reuse proven prompts so you don't start from scratch every time.

3. **Templates with variable placeholders**
   Make prompts flexible with placeholders like [PROJECT], [AUDIENCE], [TONE].

4. **Shared library creates consistent tone and quality**
   Everyone uses the best prompts, delivering consistent results.

5. **Library as a living document**
   Review, refine, and retire prompts as your needs evolve.

What you Need to Remember

Save your best prompts
Capture and store prompts that deliver great results.

Template with placeholders
Use variables like [PROJECT], [AUDIENCE], [TONE] to make prompts reusable across different needs.

Share for consistency
Share the library with your team so everyone uses aligned, high-quality prompts.

Keep your library updated
Review regularly, improve what works, and retire what no longer does.

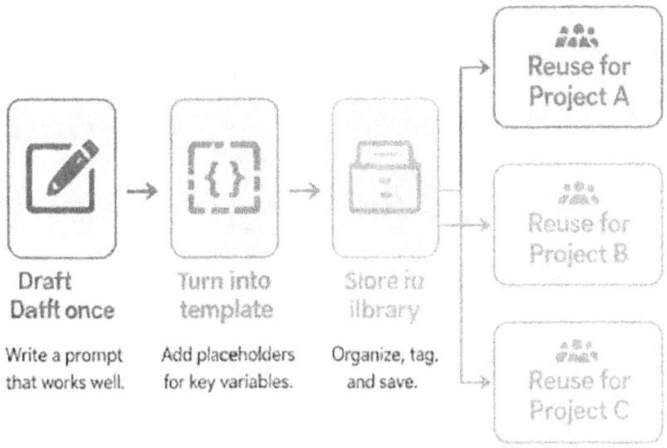

Good library tools

- Google Docs / Drive
- Notion / Coda / Confluence
- SharePoint / OneDrive
- Airtable / Monday / ClickUp

Tag templates by use case

- Marketing, Sales, Product
- HR, Support, Operations
- Research, Strategy, Finance
- Internal, External, Customer

Add date + owner for each prompt

- Date created / updated
- Who owns it
- Who to contact
- Review schedule

What Agent Mode Changes in Practice

From Chat to Agents

1 **Agents handle multi-step tasks autonomously.**
They break complex goals into steps and carry them out.

2 **AI plans sequences of actions.**
The agent decides what to do next and adapts as it goes.

3 **Agents can use tools.**
They can search the web, run code, read files, and use apps.

4 **You delegate outcomes, not prompts.**
Give the goal and constraints, not step-by-step instructions.

5 **Human role shifts to supervisor.**
You guide, review, and hold the agent accountable for results.

What you Need to Remember

Think in outcomes, not prompts
Describe the end state you want and let the agent plan the steps.

Supervise, don't micromanage
Check plans, monitor progress, and validate final outputs.

Match tools to risk
Use higher oversight when agents use powerful tools or sensitive data.

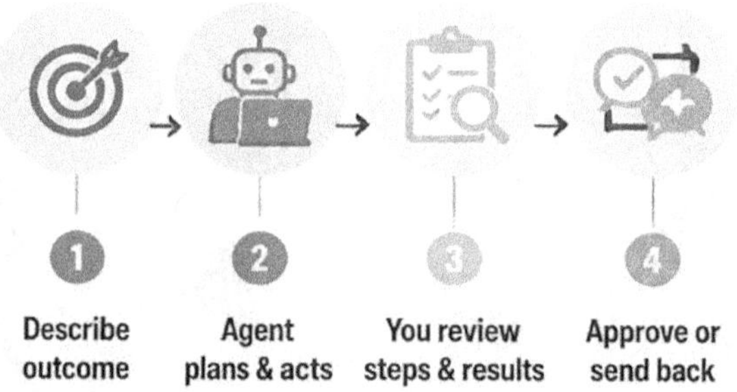

Good supervisor habits
- Ask the agent to show its plan
- Spot-check tool use
- Compare outputs to your expectations

Watch for warning signs
- Vague plans
- Missing sources or evidence
- Agent confident but wrong

Designing Safe Agent Tasks

1 Set a clear, bounded goal
- Define the task, success criteria, and what "done" looks like.
- Keep the scope tight and measurable.

2 Define access and permissions
- Grant only the data, tools, and systems the agent needs.
- Use least privilege by default.

3 Build in checkpoints
- Add review points for key milestones.
- Require confirmation before continuing or making changes.

4 Set escalation rules
- Define what triggers escalation and who gets notified.
- Route high-risk or unclear situations to a human.

5 Start with low-risk tasks
- Pilot on non-critical work first.
- Learn, refine, and expand gradually.

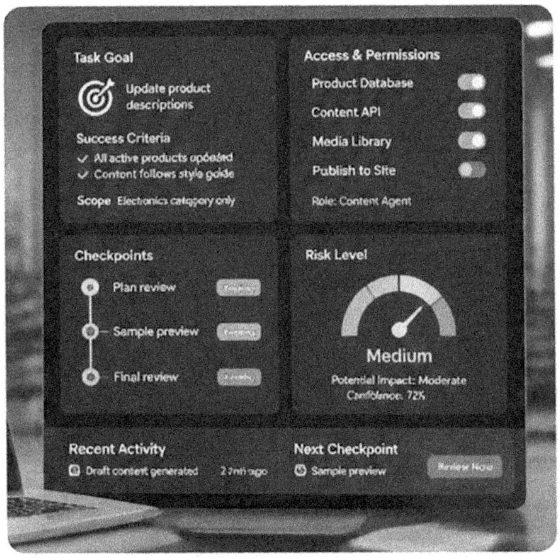

What you Need to Remember

Be specific about goals.
Clear goals reduce ambiguity and keep the agent focused on the right outcome.

Control permissions tightly.
Limit access to only what's required. Assume less and grant intentionally.

Add pause points.
Checkpoints create opportunities to catch issues early and adjust before proceeding.

Escalate real-world impact.
Route uncertain, sensitive, or high-impact situations to humans without delay.

Start small and learn.
Build confidence with low-risk tasks, measure results, and scale what works.

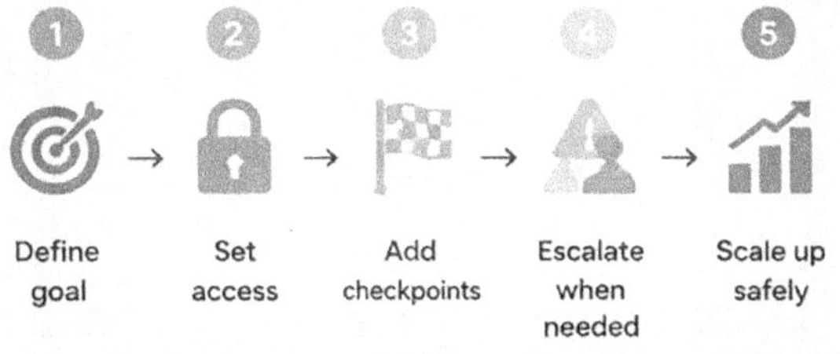

Before you start
- Is the goal clear and measurable?
- Are access and permissions minimal?
- Are success criteria defined?
- Are checkpoints and escalations set?

During the run
- Monitor progress and outputs.
- Review checkpoints on time.
- Watch risk level and signals.
- Escalate when rules are met.

Afterwards
- Did the outcome meet the goal?
- What went well or could improve?
- What should we change next time?
- Update rules and learnings.

Supervising AI Agents Effectively

Supervising day-to-day work

1. **Supervision ≠ micromanagement**
   Focus on outcomes, not every step.
2. **Review before you use**
   Check accuracy, tone, and completeness every time.
3. **Watch for recurring errors**
   Spot patterns early and fix the root cause.
4. **Fix by re-prompting**
   Clarify, add context, and iterate the prompt.
5. **Keep humans in the loop**
   Humans own the decisions and final sign-off.

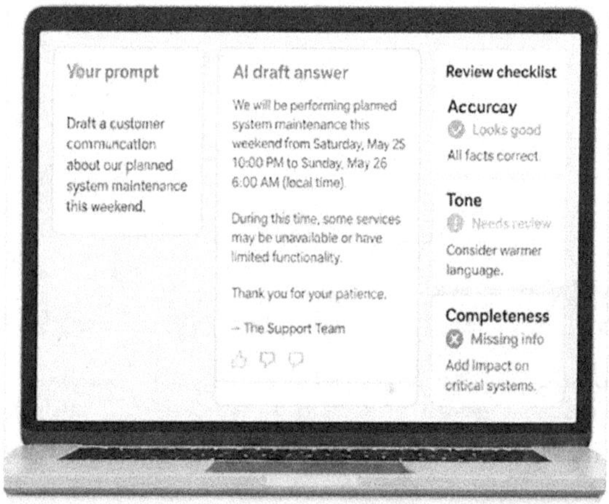

What you Need to Remember

Aim for lightweight, consistent review
Short, steady reviews prevent big problems later.

Check accuracy, tone, and completion every time
Good habits make reliable AI outputs the norm.

Design explicit human sign-off for anything that matters to stakeholders
Accountability builds trust and reduces risk.

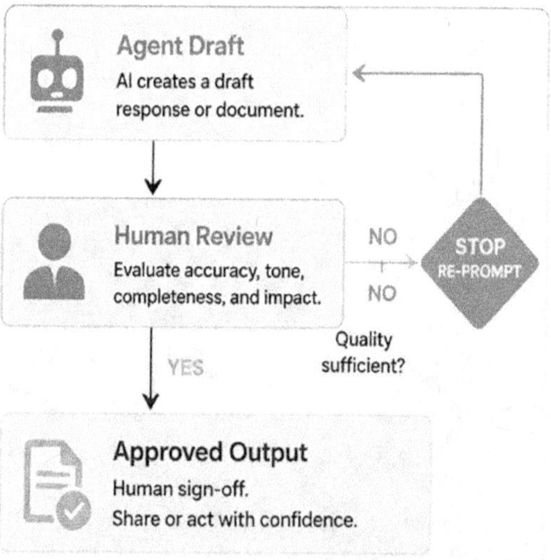

Quick checks: What decision will this drive?

Is this good enough to put my name on?

Did I improve the prompt or just fix the document?

When to Use Chat, Copilot, or Agent

Choosing the right mode

1 Chat

- Quick questions & drafts
- Explore ideas step-by-step
- You review every response

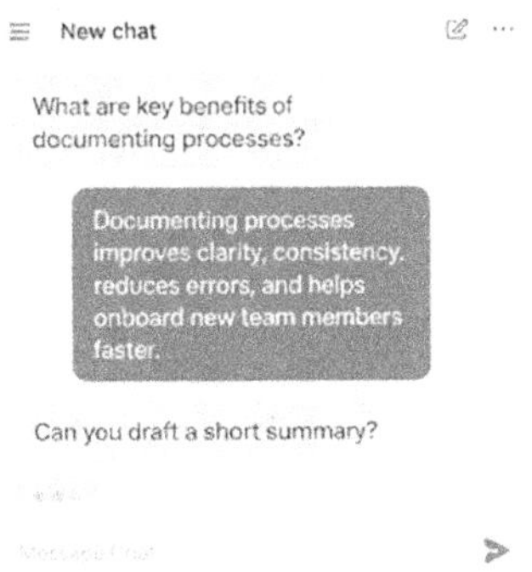

2 Copilot

- Works inside Word, Excel, Teams
- Great for editing, summarising, transforming
- You stay in the driver's seat

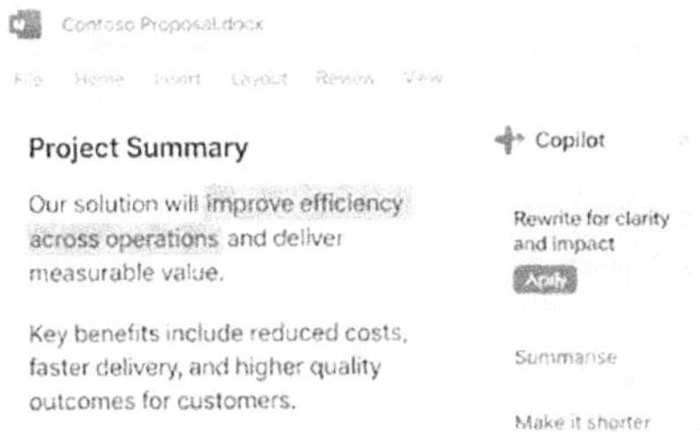

3 Agent mode

- Delegate multi-step workflows
- Clear outcome, clear constraints
- Best for repeatable processes

What you Need to Remember

Match autonomy to risk
Higher autonomy can drive scale, but only when the risk is understood and controlled.

Clarity in, oversight out
Give clear goals, constraints, and success criteria—and always review the outputs.

Unsure? Start in Chat, then upgrade to Agent for repeatable flows.
Build confidence, then build systems.

Signals to switch modes

Stuck in back-and-forth?
Move to Copilot or Agent.

Repeating the same steps?
Design an Agent.

High stakes or regulation?
Keep a human in control.

Autonomy spectrum

Where do these modes sit?

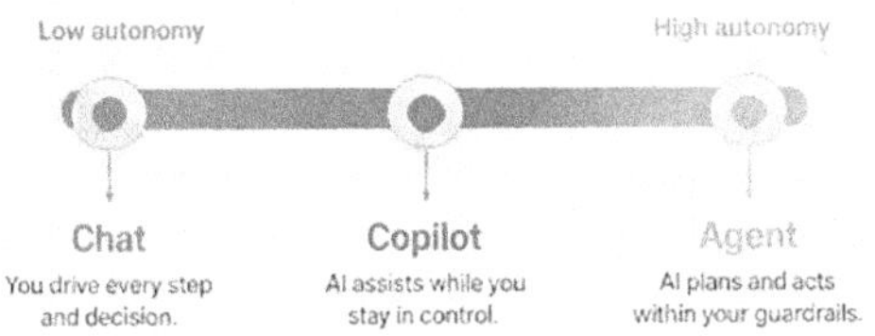

Risk vs. autonomy

Choose the right balance.

Before you start: What's the outcome and acceptable risk?

While it runs: What will you monitor?

After it runs: What will you review or change next time?

Word and Document Workflows

AI for everyday documents

1 Start from intent, not a blank page
Tell the AI what outcome you want, who it's for, and why.

2 Pick the right document types
Policies, reports, briefs, proposals, memos, slide decks, and more.

3 Draft with Copilot, ChatGPT, or Claude
Use AI to outline, draft, and expand with structure and clarity.

4 Iterate: rewrite, tighten, change tone
Ask for different versions, shorter language, or a new tone.

5 Lock it in: review, facts, approvals
Verify facts, check sources, get approvals, and publish.

What you Need tr

AI kills the blank page, not your judgement.
AI creates the first draft.
You bring the thinking.

You direct: goal, audience, tone, constraints.
Clear direction = better output.
Vague direction = generic results.

Keep ownership: check facts, adapt for your context.
AI is your co-pilot,
not the final decision maker.

Set intent	Feed inputs	AI drafts & rewrites	You review & finalise
Define outcome, audience, tone, and constraints.	Share context, documents, and key points.	AI creates drafts, expands, and refines.	Review, edit, fact-check, and finalise.

Before you start
- Define the outcome.
- Know your audience.
- List must-include points.

During drafting
- Talk to AI in short prompts.
- Provide examples.
- Iterate instead of re-writing.

Before sending
- Run a final human read.
- Check facts and links.
- Check confidentiality.

Cross-Tool Orchestration

Design the End-to-End Flow

1. Start with the whole journey: data → narrative → slides or report.
2. Use AI to turn analysis into plain-language insights, not raw tables.
3. Then reshape the story for presentations: headlines, visuals, and key messages.
4. Let each output become the next input — don't restart from scratch.
5. Judge success by the joined-up workflow, not one impressive step.

What you Need to Remember

Think in workflows, not tools.

Plan how Excel, Word, PowerPoint and AI hand off to each other so the story stays consistent.

Use native handoffs where you can.

In Microsoft 365, ask Copilot to move content directly between apps to avoid copy-paste rework.

Outside M365, chain your prompts.

Feed the output of one step into the next prompt so each stage builds on the last.

Example Orchestration Flow

Data & Analysis	AI Summary	Draft Narrative	Slide Storyboard	Final Deck / Report
Clean, analyze and find what matters.	Turn findings into clear, plain-language insights.	Shape the message into a coherent story with structure.	Translate the story into slides with visuals and key takeaways.	Polished deck or report ready to deliver and share.

- Define the start and end of the workflow.
- Decide where AI helps and where humans review.
- Save reusable prompts for each stage.

Designing a Cross-Tool Workflow for Change Deliverables

3-Stage Cross-Tool Workflow

1. **Map the deliverable backwards**
   Start with the end in mind. Define the final change deliverable and work backwards to the data you need.
2. **Stage 1 – Analyse with AI**
   Use AI to explore data, uncover patterns, and surface the insights that matter.
3. **Stage 2 – Narrate with AI**
   Turn insights into a clear, structured story that explains the why behind the change.
4. **Stage 3 – Present with AI**
   Transform the narrative into compelling slides and visuals that drive action.
5. **Review and direct at every stage**
   Check for accuracy, bias, and alignment. Steer the AI before small errors become big mistakes.

What you Need to Remember

1. **Start from the final deliverable**
   Define the change deliverable first. Work backwards to identify the data and insights you truly need.
2. **Use Analyse → Narrate → Present**
   Move in sequence to build a strong story and a clear, action-driving presentation with AI at each handoff.
3. **Review to break error chains**
   Review and correct early to prevent small mistakes from compounding through the workflow.

Analyse
Explore data and find insights
↓
REVIEW CHECKPOINT
↓
Narrate
Turn insights into a clear story
↓
REVIEW CHECKPOINT
↓
Present
Create slides and visuals that drive action
↓
REVIEW CHECKPOINT

Quick prompts for each stage

- **Analyse:** "What are the 5 strongest signals in this data?"
- **Narrate:** "Summarize the story in 3 key messages."
- **Present:** "Create 3 slides for this executive summary."

Signs your workflow is working

- Less time formatting, more time deciding
- Better stories backed by real insights
- Fewer reworks and cleaner handoffs

Drafting Change Narratives with AI

Building a Strong Change Narrative

1. **Define the story:** Why the change, what it involves, what happens next.
2. **Know your audience:** Who's affected, what they care about, what they fear.
3. **Prompt with context:** Spell out audience, channel, tone, and length for the AI.
4. **Iterate with critique:** Ask for alternatives, e.g. leadership, staff, and FAQ versions.
5. **Apply human judgement:** Check accuracy, sensitivity, and fit with organisational voice.

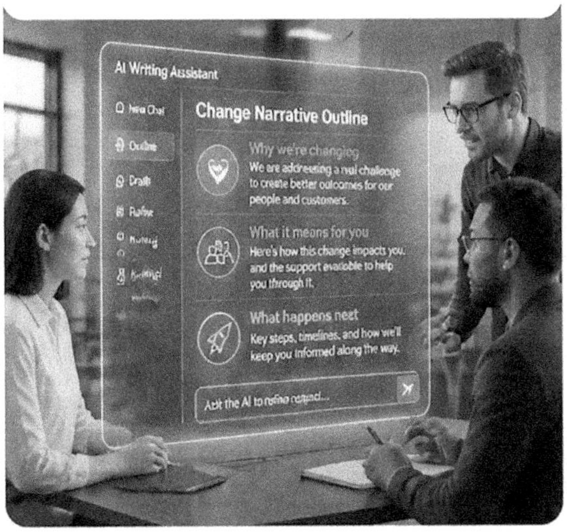

What you Need to Remember

Start with clarity: Be explicit about the problem, the change, and what success looks like.

Guide the AI: Give concrete instructions on tone, audience, examples, and format.

You are the editor: Use AI for speed and variation, but own the final message.

1. Brief the AI → 2. Generate draft → 3. Critique & refine → 4. Human sign-off

- Keep a standard prompt template for change narratives.
- Scan drafts for risk, sensitivity, and unintended signals.
- Test your narrative with a few colleagues before launch.

Policy Updates and Structured Document Revision

Using AI for Policy Revision

1. Compare policy to new rules – let AI flag gaps, conflicts, and outdated clauses.

2. Upload the current file and tell AI which sections to revise – keep headings and structure.

3. Apply across HR policies, operating procedures, and governance documents.

4. Use long-context models like Claude for full policies and annexes.

5. Keep human review: legal, risk, or SME sign-off before anything goes live.

What you Need to Remember

Start from the current policy.

Use AI to revise and compare, not to invent new rules from scratch.

Treat AI as an assistant, not the authority.

AI can map gaps and rewrite text, but humans own risk, precedent, and sign-off.

Design a clear review workflow.

Decide who checks AI drafts, how changes are approved, and where final versions are stored.

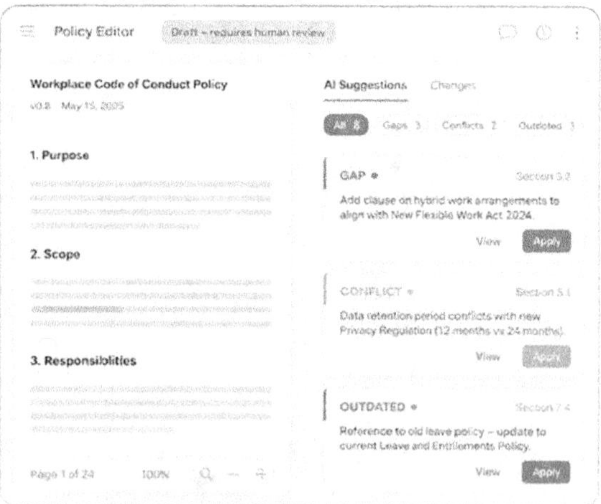

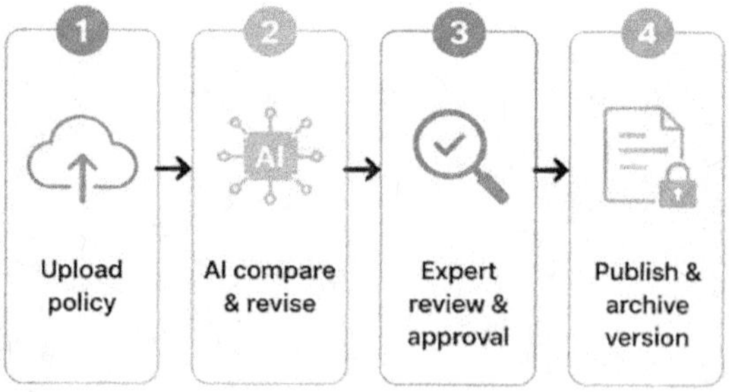

Before using AI on any policy...

- Confirm the latest regulatory source
- Strip out confidential data where possible
- Log which model and prompt you used

Stakeholder Packs and Targeted Communications

Designing Stakeholder Packs with AI

1. Tailor by stakeholder group – goals, risks, and context differ.
2. Start from one master brief; ask AI for role-specific versions.
3. Use this prompt pattern: 'Rewrite for [audience] worried about [issue], in [tone], under [word count].'
4. Generate surrounding materials: exec summary, cover email, FAQs, Q&A sheets.
5. Always review for tone, accuracy, and sensitivities before sending, especially for senior or at-risk roles.

What you Need to Remember

One source, many versions.

Keep a single master narrative and let AI adapt it for each audience.

Make the prompt do the work.

Specify audience, concern, tone, and length so outputs are targeted, not generic.

You own the message.

Scan every pack for risk, empathy, and clarity before it leaves the building.

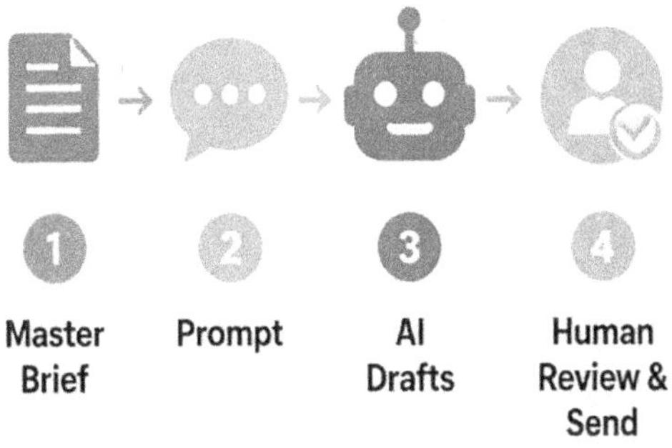

Before you generate

- Define audiences
- Clarify concerns
- Agree tone

Quick prompt tweaks

- Shorter/longer
- More formal/relaxed
- Add or remove detail

Red flag checks

- Could this upset or alarm?
- Any factual or privacy risks?
- Do leaders still sound human?

Excel and Data Workflows

Using AI with Excel and Data

1. Change programmes create rich data: surveys, readiness scores, adoption and feedback.
2. **Copilot in Excel:** ask in plain language to summarise trends, spot outliers, and build charts.
3. **ChatGPT Advanced Data Analysis and Claude:** upload spreadsheets to explore patterns and drivers.
4. High-value uses: readiness scoring, sentiment trends, benefits realisation, risk heat maps.
5. AI speeds up insight; humans still judge what it means for the programme.

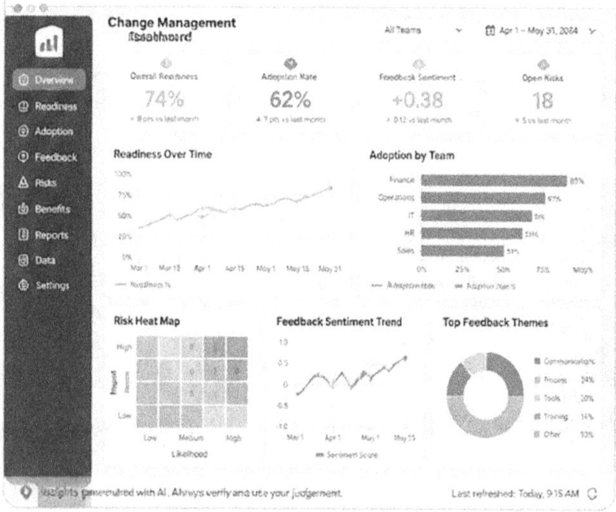

What you Need to Remember

Ask AI to do the heavy lifting.

Use Copilot, ChatGPT, and Claude for cleaning, summarising, and visualising data so you can focus on decisions, not formulas.

Stay close to the numbers.

Check sources, sense-check anomalies, and compare with what you see on the ground. If the pattern looks odd, dig deeper.

Turn insight into action.

Translate findings into clear messages, targeted support, and early risk interventions for your change programme.

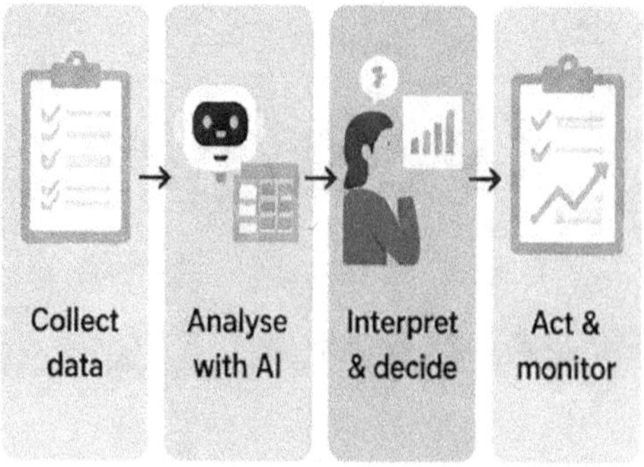

Before you start: define questions you need answered.

Protect privacy: remove personal data where possible.

Build a rhythm: review dashboards at a regular cadence.

Readiness Analysis and Sentiment Trends in Excel

Using Excel for Readiness & Sentiment

1. **Combine survey scores, capability checks, and engagement signals into one table per period.**
   Keep all readiness and sentiment data in a single, structured source.
2. **Use AI or filters to slice by team, role, or location so you see exactly who needs support.**
   Spot gaps and prioritise tailored interventions.
3. **Import survey and pulse data, then chart sentiment trends against key project dates.**
   See how sentiment moves and what drives the change.
4. **Ask Copilot in Excel to build pivots, highlight risk segments, and draft narrative summaries.**
   Save time and focus on decisions, not spreadsheets.
5. **Log qualitative reasons or flags beside scores to explain low readiness or negative sentiment.**
   Context turns numbers into meaningful action.

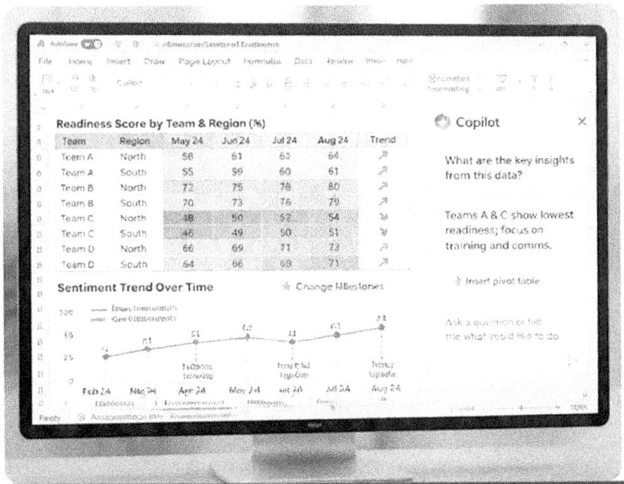

What you Need to Remember

Target support, don't generalise.

Segment readiness so leaders see which teams and roles are furthest behind and why.

Track sentiment over time.

Feed pulse surveys into Excel, chart trends, and link them to change milestones.

Pair numbers with reasons.

Combine scores, comments, and flags so every metric has a 'because' you can act on.

Collect data
↓
Clean & load into Excel
↓
Segment with AI / Copilot
↓
Visualise trends
↓
Share story with stakeholders

Quick checks
Can we see who needs help, where, and why?

Governance
Protect privacy when segmenting by team or location.

Next action
Use Copilot to draft the next readiness and sentiment update.

Benefits Tracking and Reporting with AI

Using AI for Benefits Tracking

1 **Link activity to outcomes.**
AI connects actions to real results across productivity, quality, cost, and time.

2 **Build a benefits register.**
AI structures benefits, defines baselines, targets, owners, and measurement logic.

3 **Analyze and explain variances.**
AI analyzes variance, forecasts trends, and drafts clear narratives.

4 **Report regularly, stay visible.**
AI generates reports and visuals that keep leadership informed and aligned.

5 **Keep humans in the loop.**
Change leaders validate numbers, interpret variance, and challenge assumptions.

What you Need to Remember

Make outcomes explicit.
Define what success looks like, set clear baselines, and agree on measures that matter.

Let AI do the heavy lifting.
AI can collect, organize, analyze, and visualize data at scale—faster and more consistently than manual methods.

Humans own meaning and decisions.
People provide context, judgment, and accountability. AI informs—leaders decide.

Set baselines	→ Feed data in	→ AI analyses	→ Leader interprets	→ Share story
Define what we're aiming to achieve.	Bring in data from systems and sources.	AI analyzes, finds patterns, and explains variance.	Leaders add context and decide what it means.	Share clear stories that drive action and trust.

Quick Setup Checklist

- Define 3–5 key benefits and their owners.
- Set baselines, targets, and measurement rules.
- Connect data sources and automate updates.

Signals You're on Track

- Data is fresh, complete, and consistent.
- Reports tell clear stories, not just numbers.
- Leaders use insights to make better decisions.

PowerPoint and Storytelling Workflows

Designing AI-Powered Decks

1. **Start with the story, not the slides.** Clarify audience, decision, and change you want.
2. **Use Copilot to draft.** Feed a prompt, Word doc, or outline to generate a first-pass deck and notes.
3. **Let AI clean up structure.** Ask it to reformat, group ideas, and apply a consistent visual theme.
4. **Use ChatGPT/Claude for detail.** Get slide outlines, talking points, and alternative framings.
5. **You own the narrative arc.** Adjust flow, emphasis, and tone so the journey feels believable and motivating.

What you Need to Remember

AI drafts, you decide.
Treat Copilot and chatbots as fast assistants, not final authors.

Protect the story arc.
Check that the sequence moves from problem to possibility to next steps.

Make decks feel human.
Add your examples, language, and visuals so leaders recognise their world.

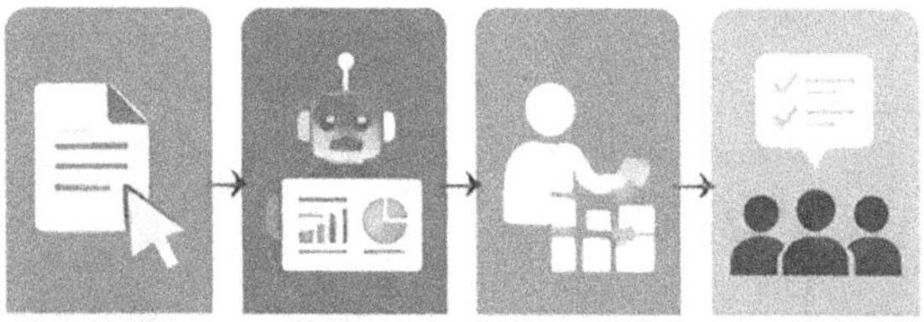

Capture source material (briefs, docs, notes) → Generate first draft with Copilot / chatbots → Edit for story, evidence, and emotion → Test with stakeholders, refine, then lock deck

Before you present, check...

- Does every slide earn its place?
- Is the 'so what?' clear for executives?
- Are next steps and owners explicit?

Set-up → Problem → Options → Decision → Next steps

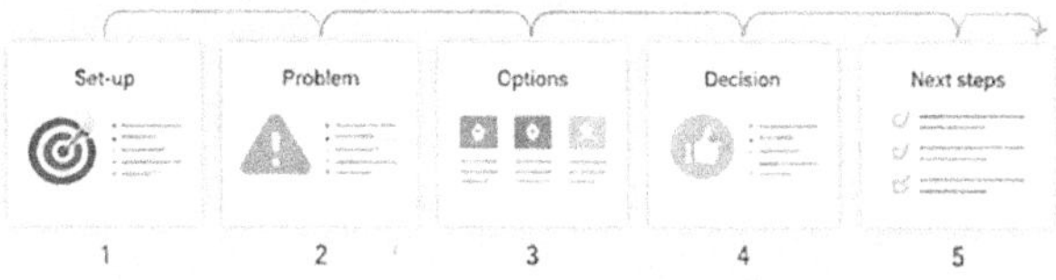

Building Executive Decks and Training Slides

Designing with AI: Exec vs Training Slides

1 Executive decks

- Keep it brief and scannable.
- Lead with the decision path.
- Focus on 3–5 key messages.
- Include supporting data, not dumps.

2 Training slides

- Start with learning objectives.
- Build complexity step by step.
- Use examples and practice to reinforce.

3 Prompting AI differently

- Ask for a concise exec summary with key decisions.
- Ask for a step-by-step lesson outline with learner activities.

4 Restructure the draft

- Review the narrative flow.
- Reorder, cut fluff, add missing pieces.
- Align to audience questions.

5 Speaker notes

- Generate notes for each slide.
- Edit for your voice and tone.
- Mark pauses and emphasis.

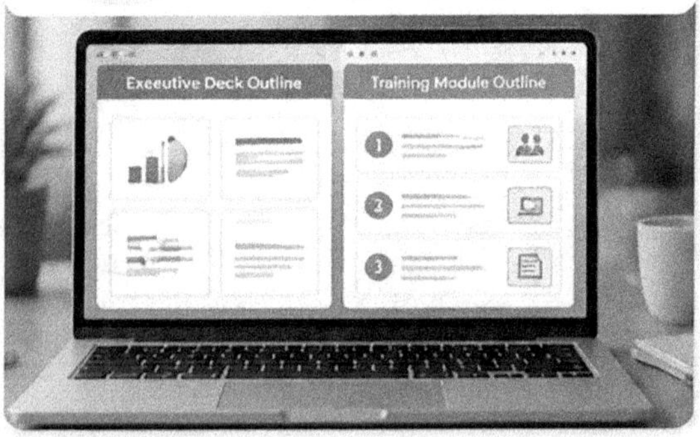

What you Need to Remember

Different goal, different structure.

Executive decks aim to drive decisions. Training slides aim to build understanding and skills. Structure should match the intent.

AI gives you a draft, not the final story.

AI can draft fast, but you bring the judgment. Always edit for logic, audience, and tone before it earns your name.

Reuse once the story is clear.

Start from a strong executive deck. Then expand it into training with context, examples, and exercises.

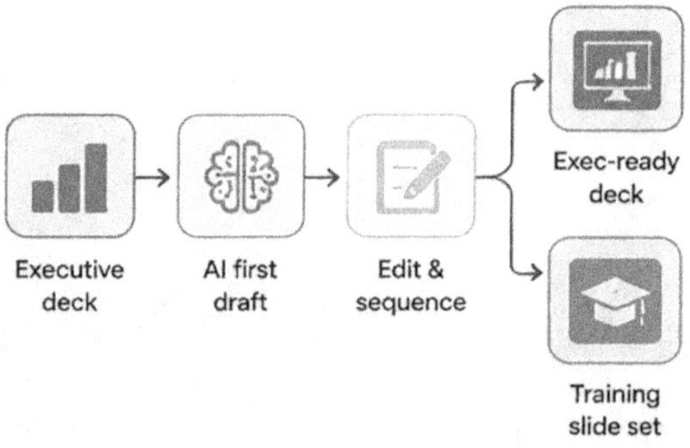

Quick AI Prompt Starters

- "Create a 5-slide executive deck outline for a leadership decision."
- "Create a training slide outline with learning objectives and activities."
- "Write speaker notes for these slides with key points, tone, and timing cues."

Checklist Before You Share

- [ ] Is the decision or outcome clear?
- [ ] Are the key messages or objectives visible?
- [ ] Does the flow make sense without you?
- [ ] Are visuals simple and intentional?
- [ ] Have you checked facts and data?

When API-Based Workflows Are Worth It

Where APIs Shine

Move beyond one-off chats: APIs let AI run in the background instead of waiting for someone to open a prompt.

Best for scale: handle large batches like surveys, logs, or feedback in one automated run, not message by message.

Great for repeatable work: similar inputs, standardised outputs, and clear logic the system can follow every time.

Trigger from your systems: form submissions, tickets, calendar events, or status changes can start AI work automatically.

Practical rule of thumb: if you reuse the same prompt several times a week, it's a good candidate for automation.

What you Need to Remember

Think in workflows, not chats –
Use APIs when the same AI step shows up again and again across your processes.

Let events start the work –
Connect AI to the tools you already use so submissions and updates kick off the flow.

Start small, automate the obvious –
Begin with one repetitive, high-volume use case and expand once it's reliable.

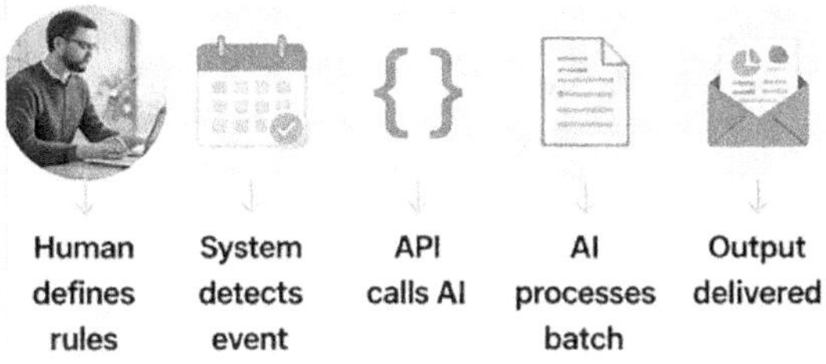

1. List 3 prompts you repeat every week.
2. Mark which have clear inputs and outputs.
3. Pick one and sketch the trigger → AI step → destination.

Simple AI Workflow Patterns

Five-Step Pattern for AI Automations

1. **Intake – how work enters**
   Capture requests from forms, emails, surveys, or system events.
2. **Classify – sort the signal**
   Use AI to tag by topic, urgency, sentiment, or audience.
3. **Draft – generate the output**
   Have AI write replies, summaries, or structured notes from the classified input.
4. **Escalate – send to people**
   Route unclear, risky, or high-impact cases to a human reviewer.
5. **Report – close the loop**
   Aggregate activity into logs, dashboards, or status updates for leaders.

What you Need to Remember

Think in patterns, not tools.
Most change-management automations can be mapped to the same five steps. Start by sketching the flow before choosing tech.

Design for human judgment.
Keep escalation points explicit. Anything ambiguous, sensitive, or high-stakes should pause for human review.

Make insight the end product.
Reporting turns many small AI tasks into useful programme insight. If leaders can't see it, it doesn't count.

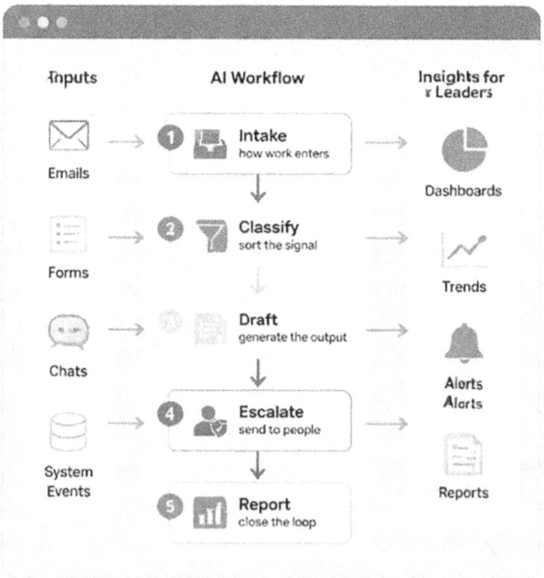

Can I describe this task with the five steps?

Where must a human step in?

What will we track and report?

Connecting AI to Enterprise Tools

Where AI Connects to Your Tools

1. **Knowledge bases**
   AI looks up policies, FAQs, and guidance before replying, so answers match real rules.

2. **Forms & intake**
   Submissions kick off AI triage: classify, prioritise, and route to the right queue.

3. **Ticketing systems**
   Drafts responses, suggests categories, and flags SLA or backlog risks.

4. **CRM platforms**
   Uses role, location, and history to personalise outreach at scale.

5. **Collaboration hubs**
   Posts summaries, alerts, and next steps into Teams or Slack instead of a separate app.

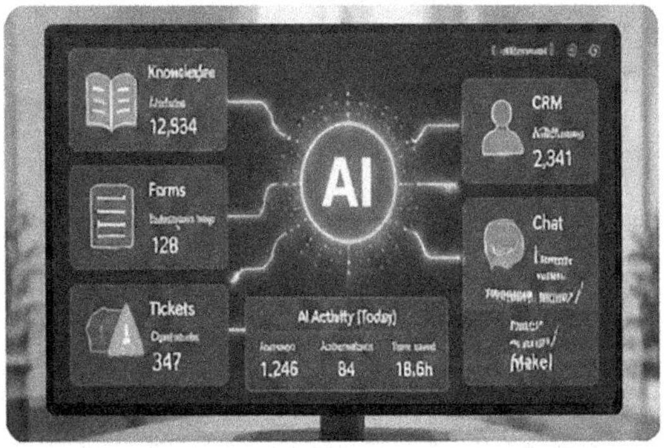

What you Need to Remember

Connect AI to real systems, not just demos.

Link it to knowledge, tickets, CRM, and collaboration tools so it works with live data.

Let workflows, not features, drive design.

Start from the journey: who submits, what gets triggered, where updates should appear.

You don't need heavy coding.

Use Power Automate, Zapier, or Make as connectors so teams can experiment safely.

User action (form, chat, email) → Connector flow (Power Automate / Zapier / Make) → AI call (model + prompt) → Update enterprise tool (KB, ticket, CRM) → Notify people (channel post, email, dashboard)

Design checklist

- Is data source trusted?
- Where is output stored?
- Who gets notified?

Risks to watch

- Out-of-date policies, wrong routing, over-reliance on drafts.

Good first pilots

- Policy Q&A bot, intake triage, meeting-summary-to-ticket flow.

From Prototype to Production

Turning an AI Prototype into a Reliable Workflow

Idea → Live Use

1 Testing on real-but-safe data

- Run on real, low-stakes cases first.
- Use messy inputs: typos, odd formats, rare cases.
- Log failures instead of fixing them on the fly.

Recent Test Runs

2 Structured output review

- Compare AI outputs with human answers.
- Note where it disagrees, not just where it's wrong.
- Use this phase to tune prompts, rules, and guardrails.

Comparison: Human | AI | Match

3 Map the edge cases

- List inputs the workflow handles badly.
- Decide: auto-reject, request more info, or send to a human.
- Make the 'we're not sure" path explicit.

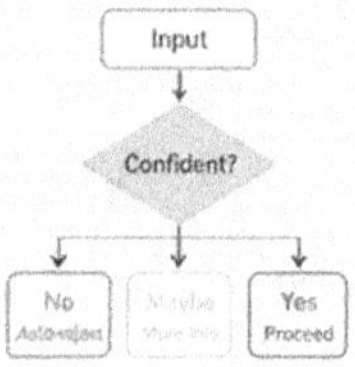

4 Monitor like a live system

- Track quality, errors, and escalations over time.
- Watch for drift: data, prompts, or upstream changes.
- Schedule regular reviews, don't rely on complaints.

Run Quality: 92% | Errors: 2.6% | Escalations | Drift Risk

5 Operational handover & change management

- Document inputs, steps, owners, and fail paths.
- Make it runnable by someone who ddin't build it.
- Explain to affected teams what's changing and why.

Handover Playbook
- Inputs & formats
- Workflow steps
- Owners & contacts
- Failure paths
- Change log

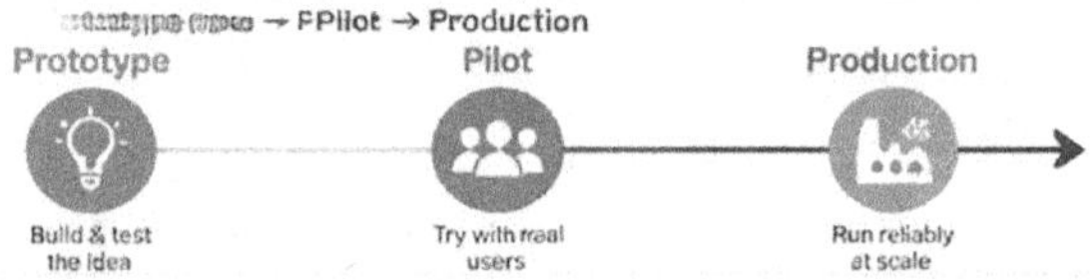

What you Need to Remember

1. Build confidence before you scale.

Use real data, human comparison, and clear edge-case rules so you know where the workflow is safe—and where it isn't.

2. Treat automation as ongoing work.

Monitor performance, retrain when inputs change, and keep a clear owner for the workflow.

3. Design for people, not just the model.

Explain how the automation works, how to challenge it, and when humans take over.

AI Operations Dashboard

● System Healthy

Run Quality: 92% ▲ 6% vs last 7 days

Escalations: 36 ▼ 12% vs last 7 days

Last Review: 2 days ago, May 12, 2025

Runs Over Time (May 6 – May 12)

Outcome Breakdown: Successful 78% · Escalated 14% · Failed 8%

Recent Runs

ID	Input Type	Outcome	Confidence	Time
#8421	Email	Success	93%	10:42 AM
#8420	Form	Escalated	61%	10:34 AM
#8419	PDF	Success	88%	10:21 AM
#8418	Email	Failed	22%	10:15 AM
#8417	Form	Success	91%	10:02 AM

View all runs

Before launch: tested on real data, edge cases mapped.

In production: monitor quality and drift.

With people: explain changes, invite feedback.

SECTION 3

Applying AI Across the Change Lifecycle

This section follows the change lifecycle from first discovery through to embedded adoption, applying AI at each stage. It begins with discovery and readiness assessment, using AI for stakeholder discovery that maps groups, interests, and influence, sentiment and feedback analysis across surveys, comments, and meetings, readiness scoring that surfaces friction before rollout, and baseline assessment of current skills and AI maturity. It then moves to strategy and change design, where AI supports developing the strategy, framing objectives, mapping impacts across the organisation, defining success measures that genuinely capture change, scenario planning and option testing, audience segmentation, and designing the future workflow with AI built into it.

The next part covers communications, engagement, and training, including personalised communication design and role-specific messaging, AI-supported manager toolkits and talk tracks, AI-generated learning content with proper quality control, and conversational support channels that move from static FAQs to adaptive internal assistants.

The final part concerns adoption, reinforcement, and measurement, covering how to measure behaviour change with AI, build adoption dashboards and narrative reporting, run continuous improvement loops, and track value realisation and benefits. The consistent theme is that AI adds value at every phase, but only when its outputs are checked and tied to real behaviour rather than activity. By the end you should be able to weave AI through discovery, design, delivery, and reinforcement, strengthening each stage while keeping human judgement and accountability at the centre of the programme.

AI-Assisted Stakeholder Discovery | Mapping groups, interests, and influence patterns

Using AI to map your stakeholders

1. **Start with rich inputs**
   Upload org charts, project briefs, governance decks, and recent meeting notes so AI can see the whole landscape.

2. **Ask for stakeholder hypotheses**
   Prompt the AI with the change goals, key roles, and business context to generate a draft list of impacted groups and individuals.

3. **Spot hidden influencers**
   Use AI to look for connectors, long-tenured experts, and informal leaders that don't appear on formal plans.

4. **Turn outputs into planning assets**
   Export results straight into influence-interest grids, engagement plans, and tailored communication lists.

5. **Validate with humans, not hope**
   Review the AI map with people who know the organisation and refine before you act.

What you Need to Remember

AI gives you speed, not certainty.

Treat outputs as a strong first draft; decisions still sit with people who understand the politics and culture.

Focus on relationships, not just roles.

Pay attention to who trusts whom, where resistance might sit, and where champions can amplify the change.

Close the loop before acting.

Sense-check the map with sponsors and local leaders, adjust, then lock in your engagement and communication plan.

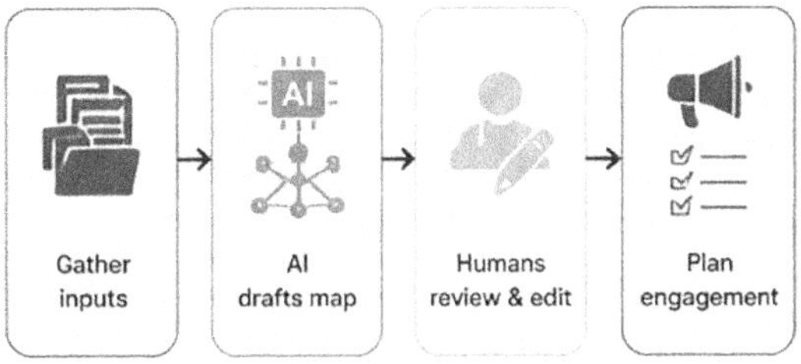

Quick checks before you trust the map

- Did we include the messy, informal reality?
- Have the right leaders reviewed this?
- Do we know who might resist and who can champion?

Update the stakeholder map at each major project milestone, not just once at the start.

Sentiment and Feedback Analysis | Reading surveys, comments, and meeting outputs at scale

Making sense of feedback at scale

1. **Volume problem**
   Qualitative feedback comes from many places and in many formats.
2. **AI sentiment classification**
   AI classifies feedback sentiment across surveys, comments, and workshop notes.
3. **Theme detection and grouping**
   AI detects and groups themes across departments and roles.
4. **Trend analysis over time**
   AI tracks sentiment over time to spot improving, worsening, or flat trends.
5. **Fast AI summaries**
   AI generates concise summaries to brief leaders and adapt comms quickly.
6. **Data quality warning**
   AI outputs are only as good as the input data.

What you Need to Remember

A **Use AI to structure, not replace judgement.**

AI organises insights, but humans provide context and make decisions.

B **Act on signals quickly, before resistance hardens.**

Timely action builds trust and prevents small issues from growing.

C **Design good data in: clear questions, diverse voices, honest comments.**

Better input leads to better insights and better outcomes.

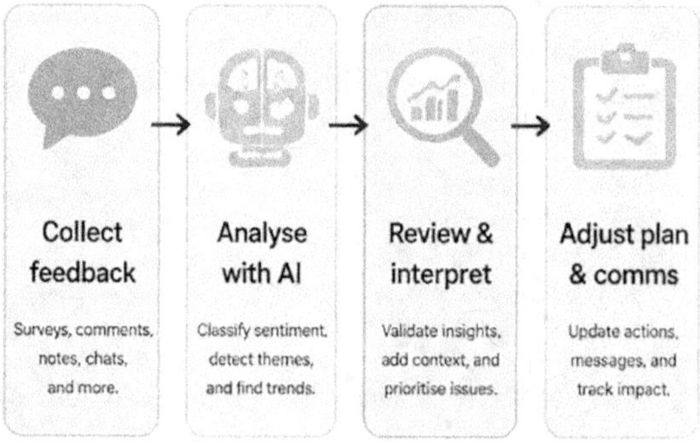

Good prompts for analysis

- What themes are emerging by team or role?
- What's getting better or worse over time?
- Which comments signal urgent risk?

Signals you're using this well

- Leaders change plans based on insights
- Employees see issues acknowledged quickly
- Sentiment trends match what people report in meetings

3.1 Discovery and Readiness Assessment

Readiness Scoring and Risk Signals | Identifying friction before rollout

Turning signals into a readiness score

1. Move beyond only interviews & workshops – useful, but slow and inconsistent at scale.
2. Let AI pull signals from surveys, usage logs, feedback and past adoption data.
3. Score key dimensions: capability, willingness to change, leadership alignment, system access.
4. Automatically flag low scores, contradictions or outlier groups for follow-up.
5. Use scores to decide: go, hold, phase rollout, or focus remediation before launch – always sense-check with local insight.

Readiness view: one page for where to lean in before rollout.

What you Need to Remember

Readiness = many signals, one story.

Combine qualitative insight with AI-generated scores so leaders see a clear, comparable picture across teams.

Treat scores as a conversation starter.

Use low scores and outliers to ask better questions, not to punish. Check for data gaps or local context before acting.

Act early on friction.

Use risk signals to adjust timing, add training and support, or split the rollout. Aim to solve issues before they appear at go-live.

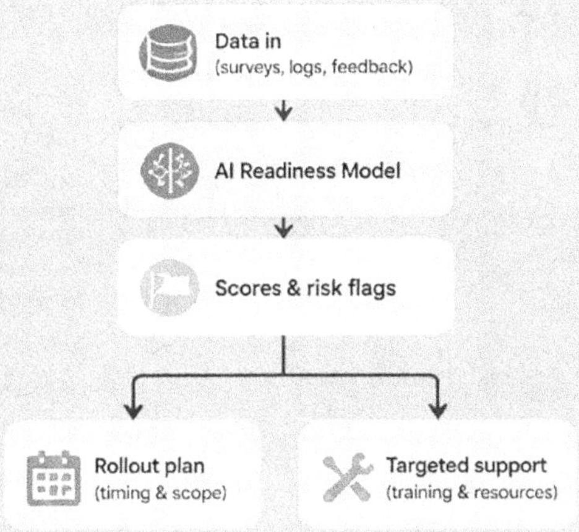

Minimum viable scorecard

- 4–6 dimensions
- simple 1–5 scale

Who must see the scores?

- local leaders
- project team
- sponsors

Keep it honest

- refresh data often
- log overrides with reasons

Baseline Capability Assessment | Understanding current skills and AI maturity

Designing a Baseline Capability Assessment

1

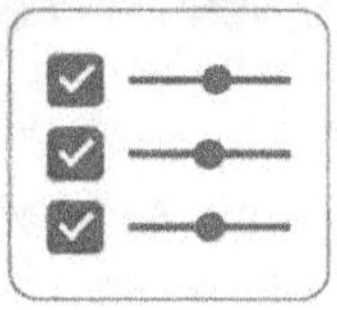

Clarify what you're measuring

Digital literacy, AI familiarity, confidence with tools, learning preferences.

2

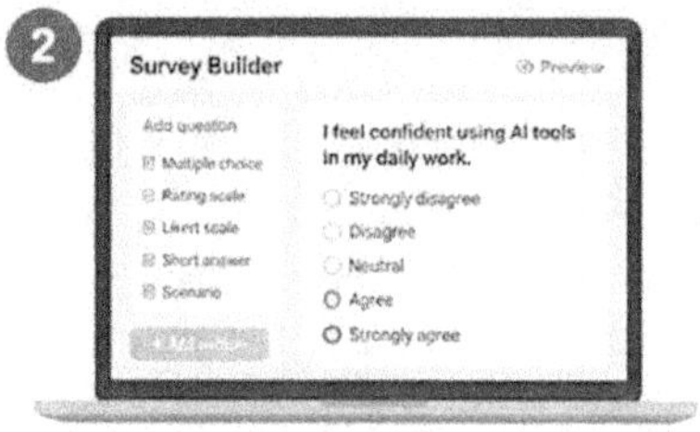

Co-design the instruments

Use AI to draft surveys, self-assessments and realistic scenarios that surface real behaviour, not just opinions.

3

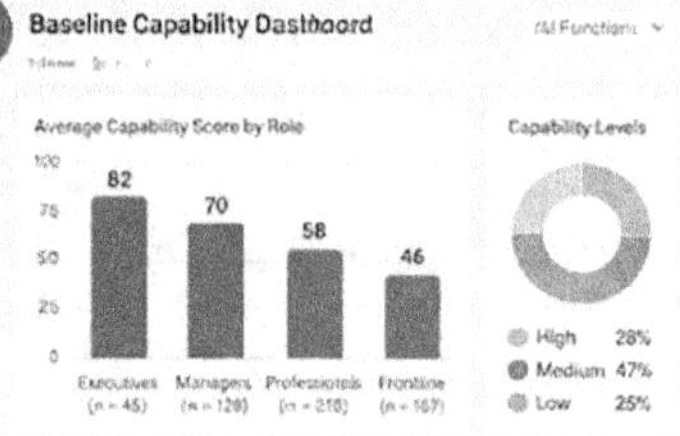

Segment the results

Slice data by role, function, location and seniority to reveal capability gaps and high-need groups.

4

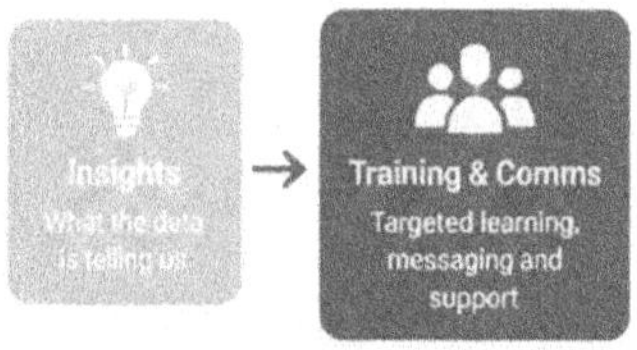

Turn insights into action

Let findings drive training depth, communication tone and where you place extra support.

5

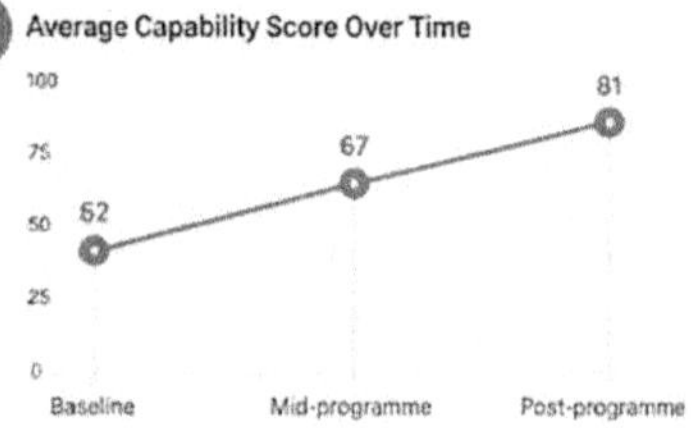

Measure progress over time

Repeat the assessment at key milestones to show measurable capability growth.

What you Need to Remember

Start from reality, not assumptions.

Use data on current skills and comfort levels so change plans match where people really are.

Let the assessment shape the journey.

Design training, messaging, and support intensity directly from what the baseline reveals.

Prove that skills are growing.

Re-run the same assessment so you can show leaders and teams that AI capability is improving.

1 Ask | **2 Analyse** | **3 Act**

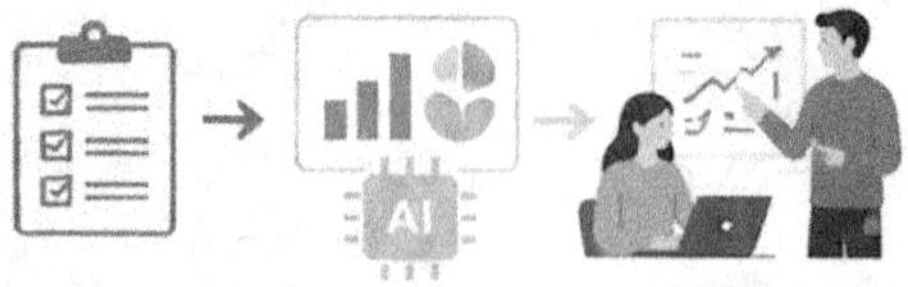

Ask: Gather honest responses about skills, confidence and

Analyse: Use AI to uncover patterns, gaps and high-need audiences.

Act: Tailor training, messaging and support to drive real capability growth.

Good prompts for building assessments

- What do people need to do with AI?
- Where do they feel least confident?
- What support would help them try new tools?

Signals you've got a strong baseline

- Leaders quote the data in decisions
- Training plans differ by audience
- Teams ask to see their progress.

Keep it ethical

- Explain how data will be used
- Offer anonymity where possible
- Share headline results back with participants.

AI-Assisted Change Strategy Development

Building the Change Strategy

1. **Set clear objectives and outcomes.**
   Define what success looks like and why it matters.
2. **Use AI to structure and expand ideas.**
   Organize options, identify gaps, and uncover new possibilities.
3. **Map impacts across people, process, tech, and culture.**
   Understand who is affected and how.
4. **Define behaviour-based success measures.**
   Focus on the behaviours that drive results.
5. **Apply human judgement and refine relentlessly.**
   Challenge assumptions and improve the strategy.

What you Need to Remember

AI speeds the thinking, not the judgement.
AI can analyze and suggest—humans decide what is right.

Define objective, impact, and evidence.
Clear goals, understood impacts, and solid evidence create better strategies.

Treat AI outputs as drafts to challenge.
Question, test, and refine before you act.

AI-Assisted Strategy Loop

Gather stakeholder inputs
↓
Ask AI to structure & stretch thinking
↓
Decide objectives, impacts, measures
↓
Document and share the strategy

Good prompts to try

- What objectives align to our strategic priorities?
- What are the biggest risks and blind spots?
- What alternative strategies should we consider?

Signals your strategy is robust

- Clear outcomes and success measures
- Evidence-based impact assessment
- Stakeholders are informed and aligned

Watch-outs

- Over-reliance on AI suggestions
- Biased or incomplete data
- Vague objectives and unmeasurable outcomes

Redefining Work with AI in the Process

Designing Workflows with AI

1 Cut low-value effort, don't add extra tools
Remove steps that don't add value before introducing AI.

2 Spot repetitive, slow, or error-prone tasks
Focus on work that consumes time or invites mistakes.

3 Free people for judgement, relationships, strategy
Shift time from doing to thinking, deciding, and creating impact.

4 Co-design with people who do the work
Involve frontline teams to design workflows that actually work.

5 Document and test the future workflow
Make the new way visible, test it, and iterate.

What you Need to Remember

Start with where time really goes
Understand how work is done today so you can redesign what matters most.

Prototype the new workflow with AI in the loop
Test quickly, learn fast, and refine based on real results.

Involve frontline experts to catch edge cases
The people closest to the work know what can go wrong—and how to fix it.

Current work	AI handles	Humans focus on
Collect data	Manages emails & requests	Decisions
Manual entry	Data entry & updates	Relationships
Find information	Summarises & creates drafts	Strategy
Draft content		
Send updates		
Report status		
File & store		

Continuous feedback improves outcomes

Quick checks
- Did we remove busywork?
- Is human judgement clear?
- Do people know the new flow?

Good inputs
Use time-logs, workflow maps, and real stories, not guesses.

Signals you're on track
Less rework, faster turnaround, and staff saying 'this feels easier'.

Framing Objectives with AI Support

Turn vague goals into AI-ready objectives

1. **Spot vague objectives**
   Phrases like "embed a culture of innovation" don't guide decisions.

2. **Feed AI the full context**
   Provide change, audience, timeline, and business driver so AI has the full picture.

3. **Ask for outcome-style objectives**
   Outcomes should be specific, measurable, and time-bound—so progress is clear.

4. **Challenge assumptions with AI**
   Ask AI to probe weak spots with: "What would have to be true for this objective to be achievable?"

5. **Iterate until it matches reality**
   Refine the objective until constraints and dependencies are visible and realistic.

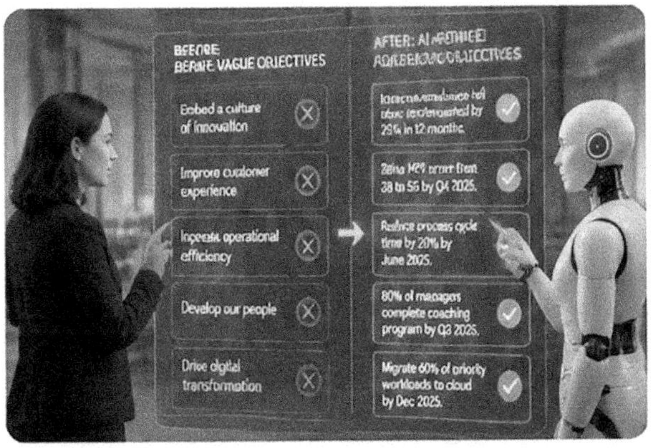

What you Need to Remember

Good objectives guide real decisions

Clear, outcome-focused objectives help leaders prioritise, allocate resources, and course-correct with confidence.

Context makes AI useful

The more complete and honest the context, the better AI can shape objectives that fit your reality.

Test feasibility before you commit

Use AI to surface risks, dependencies, and assumptions—so you set objectives you can actually achieve.

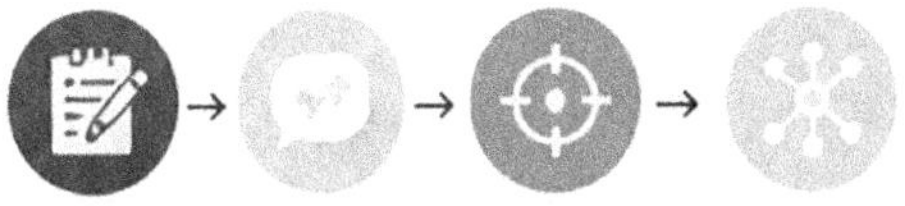

Quick prompts to try

- Tighten this goal into a specific, measurable, time-bound objective."
- What risks or assumptions could block this objective?"
- What would success look like in 12 months?"

Signals you've framed it well

- People know what success looks like.
- You can say clearly what will be different in 6–12 months.
- Leaders can act on it with confidence.

Mapping Impacts Across the Organisation

Building an AI Impact Map

1 Identify who's affected

Define the stakeholders, groups, and roles impacted by the change.

2 Map impacts across people / process / technology / culture

Explore impacts in four dimensions to capture the full picture.

3 Use AI to expand and challenge assumptions

Generate additional impacts, uncover blind spots, and test alternative perspectives.

4 Add organisational context and politics

Layer in history, power dynamics, incentives, risks, and likely resistance.

5 Turn the map into actions and interventions

Prioritise high-impact areas and design tailored actions that stick.

Example AI Impact Map

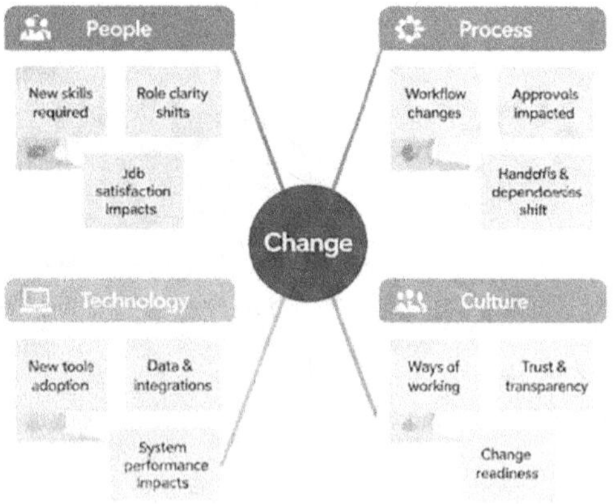

What you Need to Remember

1 AI gives you the scaffold

AI can generate a multi-dimensional impact map fast, surfacing patterns, connections, and unintended consequences.

2 You supply the context

Only you understand the politics, history, incentives, and resistance that shape real-world outcomes.

3 Co-create with stakeholders

Validate the map with those affected, refine it together, and keep it living as the change evolves.

AI Impact Mapper – Example

1. Your prompt

Map the impacts of implementing an AI-powered claims processing tool in our organisation.

- Scope: Organisation-wide
- Change type: Technology implementation
- Stakeholders: Claims team, Ops, IT, Customers, Compliance
- Time horizon: 18 months

Generate map

2. AI-generated impact map

People	Process	Technology	Culture
New AI skills needed	Faster claims triage	New AI tool adoption	Greater automation mindset
Roles will evolve	Straight-through processing increases	Data quality critical	Trust in AI needs building
Training & upskilling required	Escalation criteria shift	System integrations required	Cross-team collaboration essential
Workload rebalancing	KPIs & SLAs need update	Model bias & fairness risk	Change fatigue risk
Job security concerns	Audit & quality checks change	Security & privacy implications	Customer experience expectations
+ Add note	+ Add note	+ Add note	+ Add note

3. Next steps

Review & validate with stakeholders → Prioritise top impacts → Design tailored interventions

Before you start: write a 3–5 line change brief.

During mapping: challenge what's missing.

Afterwards: prioritise hotspots for tailored interventions.

Defining Success Measures That Actually Measure Change

Designing Metrics That Show Real Behaviour Change

1. **Focus on behaviour, not busywork.**
Track what people actually do differently, not emails sent or hours logged.

2. **Separate leading and lagging indicators.** (NOW — LATER)
Ask AI to label early signals vs end outcomes so you can react faster.

3. **Metrics for each stakeholder group.**
Use AI to propose measures for leaders, managers, front line, customers.

4. **Test every metric with a data question.**
Challenge AI: 'How would we collect this, how often, from which system?'

5. **Keep a short, sharp metric set.**
Prioritise a small list that leadership will read and act on.

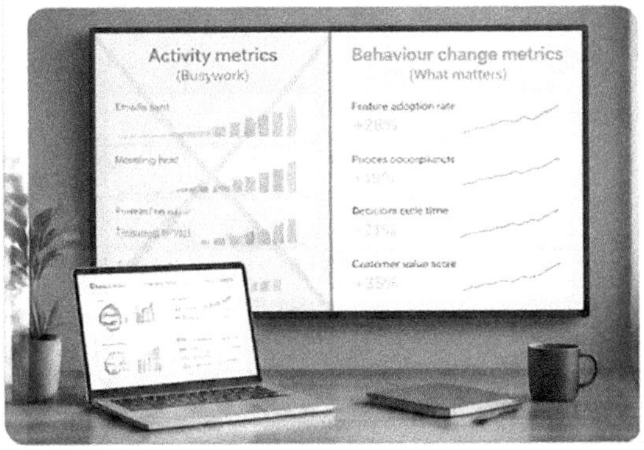

What you Need to Remember

Start with the story of change.

Describe the behaviour shift you want, then design measures that would prove it's happening.

Use AI as a metric generator, not the judge.

Let AI suggest options, then refine by feasibility, stakeholder, and leading vs lagging balance.

Tie metrics to real-world data flows.

Confirm where each metric lives, who owns it, and how often it's reviewed so action follows quickly.

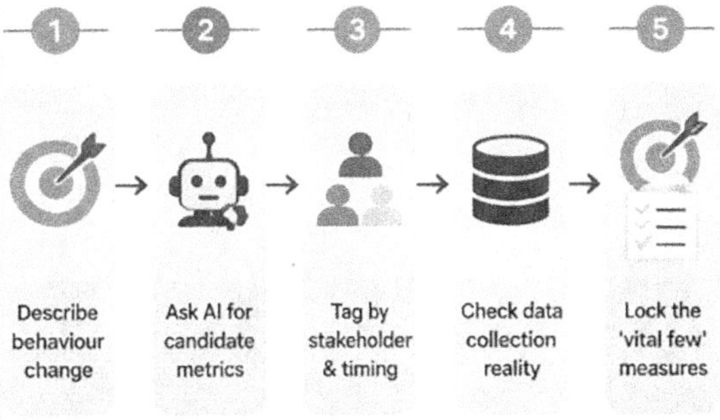

Quick Checks for Your Measurement Plan

- Would this metric change what we do next week?
- Can we see early movement, not just end results?
- Is at least one person accountable for each metric?

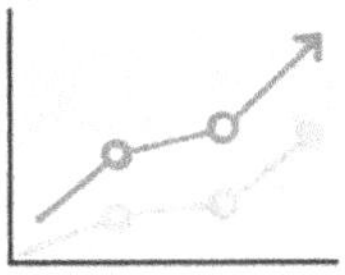

Scenario Planning and Option Testing

Using AI for Scenario Planning

1. **Test strategy under different futures**
2. **Ask AI for contrasting scenarios:** fast adoption, slow adoption, resistance, resource squeeze
3. **For each scenario, explore impact on** comms, training, timelines
4. **Use AI to surface dependencies, bottlenecks, and hidden risks**
5. **Capture no-regret moves that work across most scenarios.**

What you Need to Remember

Don't predict — prepare.

Explore multiple futures so you have options when change happens.

Stress-test before you commit.

Challenge your plan against different scenarios to expose weak spots early.

Turn insights into concrete contingencies.

Convert what you learn into clear actions you can execute quickly.

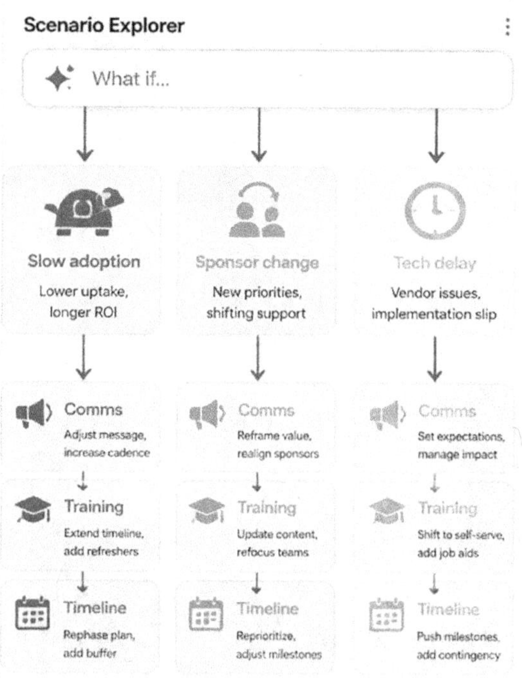

Capture top 3 risks per scenario

Review scenarios at each major milestone

Share key 'no-surprises' insights with sponsors.

Exploring Risks, Dependencies, and Trade-offs

Using AI to surface risks and dependencies

1. Most risks are human and relational, not only technical.
2. Ask AI to draft a risk register from your change brief, then refine it with the team.
3. Have AI map dependencies across workstreams, timelines, and stakeholders.
4. Use AI to list what each option improves and what it compromises.
5. Keep humans accountable for choices; AI just organises the evidence.

Risk Register (AI Assistant) — AI suggests new risks

Risk	Cause	Impact	Owner	Mitigations
		High		
		Medium		
		Medium		
		Low		

What you Need to Remember

Start with a broad risk scan.

Use AI to surface relational, process, and dependency risks early.
Then validate and prioritise with people who own the work.

Make dependencies visible.

Ask AI to sketch timelines and cross-team links so you can see where slippage or misalignment will hurt delivery.

Structure, don't outsource, decisions.

Use AI to frame options, trade-offs, and assumptions.
Senior leaders still choose – and stay accountable.

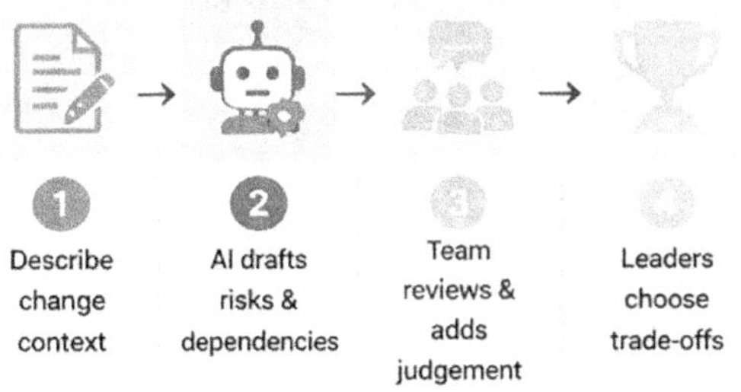

Good prompts to try

- Draft a risk register for this change initiative
- Map dependencies between these workstreams
- Compare pros and cons of these rollout options

Signals you're managing risk well

- Few 'surprise' issues late in delivery
- Dependencies tracked and owned
- Trade-off decisions documented.

Avoid

- Letting AI 'decide' on strategy
- Ignoring relational and political risks
- Treating the first AI draft as final

Audience Segmentation and Tailoring

Designing Segmented Interventions

1 Different people react differently to change.

Change impacts vary based on role, context, experience, and proximity to the change.

2 Use AI to generate realistic change personas.

AI can synthesize role data and change impact to create lifelike personas with goals, worries, and preferences.

3 Segment by what matters.

Common criteria include: impact, awareness, readiness, and proximity to change.

4 Use personas to design better experiences.

Map each persona's journey, barriers, and motivators to shape the right messages, support, and timing.

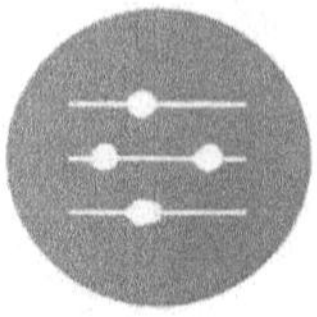

5 Tailoring ≠ more work. It's smarter work.

Targeted messages drive more engagement and better outcomes than one-size-fits-all approaches.

What you Need to Remember

One size doesn't fit all

People experience change differently. Tailored approaches lead to greater understanding, trust, and adoption.

Use AI to hear every perspective

AI helps uncover hidden concerns and preferences so no voice is missed in your planning.

Design from the most affected groups

Prioritize those with the highest impact or lowest readiness to reduce risk and build momentum.

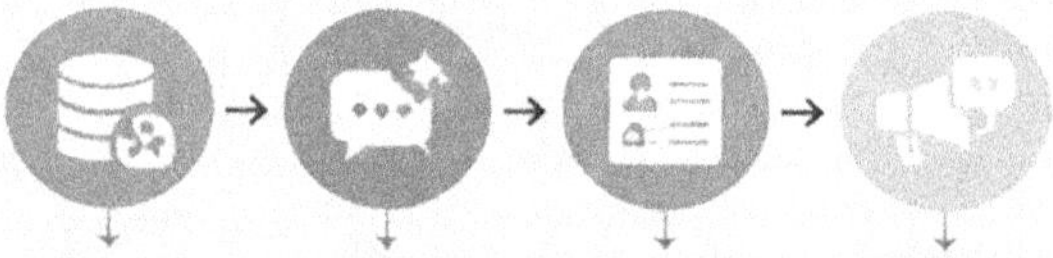

Roles & impact data	AI persona prompts	Persona profiles	Targeted comms & training
Collect role, impact level, and context.	Use AI to create persona prompts and scenarios.	Generate rich personas with goals, worries, and preferences.	Deliver the right, message, format, and support.

Quick checklist

- Mapped key groups
- Defined segmentation criteria
- Created AI personas
- Linked to actions & channels

Inputs for your AI prompt

- Roles & responsibilities
- Impact level of the change
- Top worries or concerns
- Preferred channels & formats

Signals it's working

- Fewer blanket messages and escalations
- Higher engagement from priority groups

Designing Interventions for Different User Groups

Match interventions to each segment

1. Start with readiness, capability, motivation
2. High-readiness: less talk, more enablement
3. Low-readiness or resistant: reassurance and leadership support
4. Use AI to design a menu: comms, training, coaching, job aids
5. Filter options by impact vs effort

What you Need to Remember

Design by segment, not average user

People have different needs, constraints, and mindsets. Tailor interventions to what each group requires to move forward.

Balance ambition with operational reality

Great ideas only work if they fit the time, tools, and pressures your teams actually face. Keep it practical and achievable.

Ask AI for options, you choose what's feasible.

AI can surface many possibilities. Your judgement decides what will create real change.

- Segment users
- Ask AI for options
- Rank by impact & effort
- Commit to a small set

Check: Do we know what this group really needs?

Choose: 1–3 interventions per segment, max

Review: Drop low-impact work quickly.

Designing the Future Workflow

Designing the Future Workflow

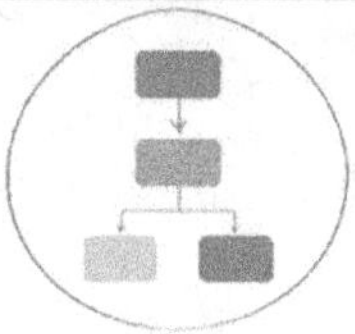

1. Define how work happens once change is embedded.

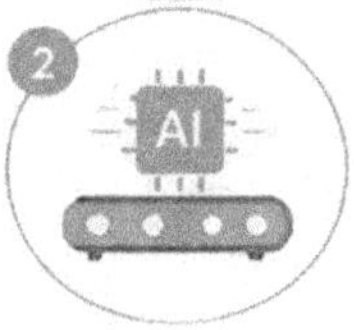

2. Design AI into the workflow – not as a bolt-on.

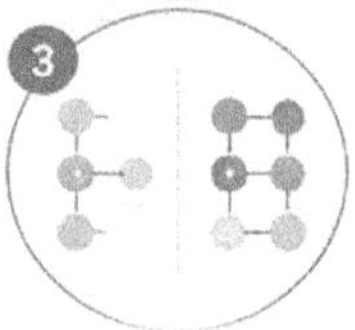

3. Map today's process, then redesign with new tools and behaviours.

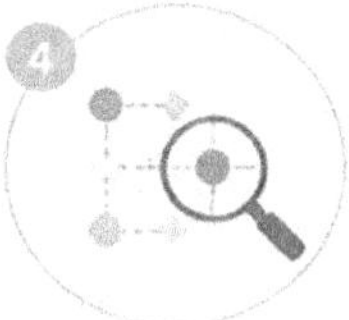

4. Target high-value AI moments: research, drafting, analysis, summarising.

5. Treat the future workflow as the bridge from strategy to day-to-day work.

What you Need to Remember

Redesign the work, not just the tool training.

Map tasks step by step and decide how work should run once AI is normal.

Ask where AI makes work easier.

For each step, check if AI can make it faster, better, or lower effort.

Make the new workflow the target model.

Align training, comms, and coaching to the redesigned process, not the old one.

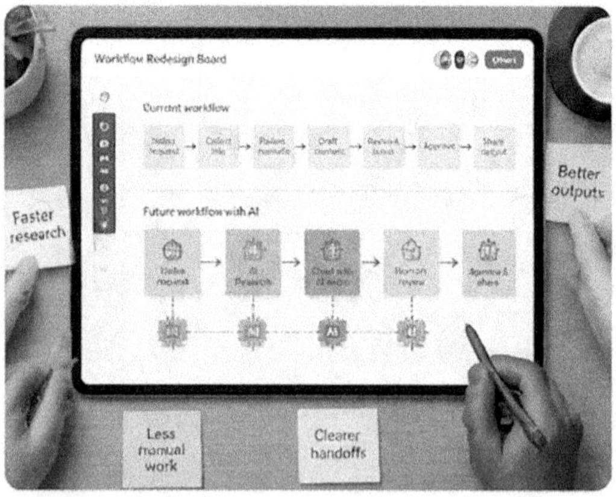

The future workflow design loop

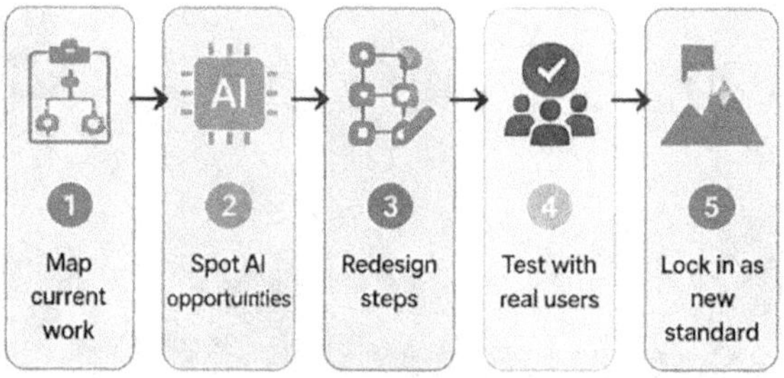

Quick prompts for workshops

- Where does work currently slow down?
- Which steps could AI safely improve?
- What will people stop doing once this workflow is live?

Signals you've nailed the future workflow

- People follow the new steps without reminders.
- AI is used at the same points every time, not ad-hoc.
- Teams say the work feels smoother, not just 'more digital'.

Personalised Communication Design

Designing role-based messages with AI

1. **One size doesn't fit all.**
   Link each role to a specific narrative and outcome.
2. **Use AI to segment at scale.**
   Group by role, impact level, concerns, and location.
3. **Capture the right inputs.**
   Role, impact, concerns, and preferred channels go into the prompt.
4. **Generate a suite of assets.**
   Emails, FAQs, manager briefs, team talk tracks, and one-pagers.
5. **Human review is the final filter.**
   You refine tone, fix gaps, and approve before sending.

What you Need to Remember

1 Start with roles, not one master email.

Define who's affected and what they care about before you write. Let AI draft per-role messages instead of forcing one generic story.

2 Turn inputs into a repeatable prompt.

Bake role, impact, concerns, and channel into a simple template the whole team can reuse for every change.

3 AI drafts, humans decide.

Keep humans accountable for tone, accuracy, and risk. Nothing goes out without a quick review and sign-off.

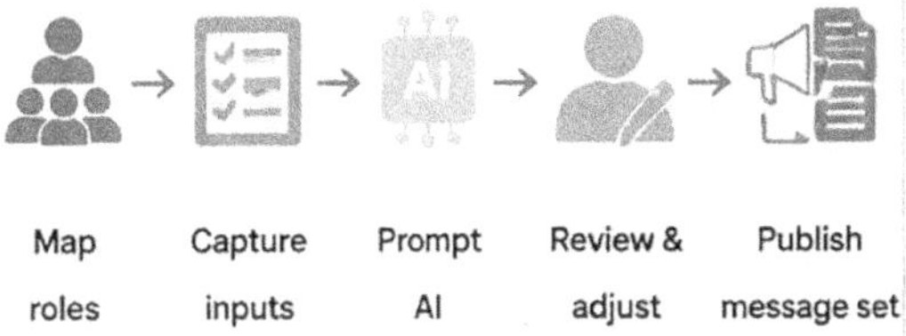

Quick checks before you send

- Does each role see 'what this means for me'?
- Have we answered likely questions and concerns?
- Is the call to action clear for every audience?

Signals it's working

- Fewer cllarification emails from managers
- Teams reuse role-based templates
- Feedback mentions 'clear and relevant' updates.

Conversational Support Channels

Using Conversational Support Channels

1. **Support at point of work**
   Answers when people are stuck in the workflow.
2. **Internal AI assistants**
   Internal AI gives instant, consistent responses.
3. **Use cases**
   Great for FAQs, process steps, policy look-ups, onboarding.
4. **Verified content**
   Grounded in current, programme-specific content.
5. **Reduced burden / better experience**
   Frees central teams for complex, human conversations.

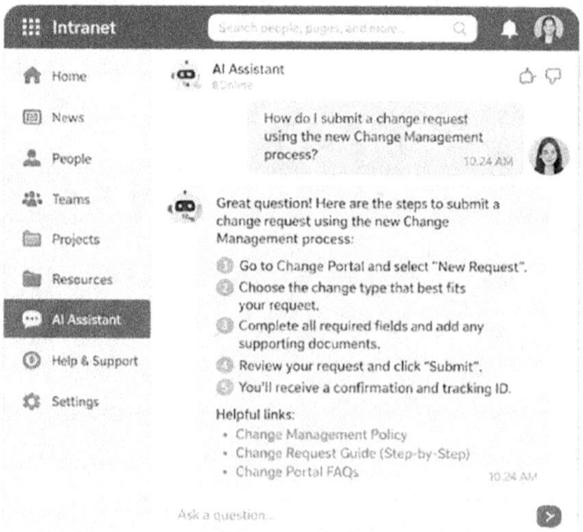

What you Need to Remember

Support at the point of need

Help is available 24/7 right inside the tools people already use.
No tickets. No waiting.

Ground assistants in trusted content

Use vetted, programme-specific sources to ensure accurate, relevant answers. Keep content current.

Let AI handle volume, humans handle nuance

Route routine questions to AI for fast, consistent answers.
Reserve specialists for complex or sensitive issues.

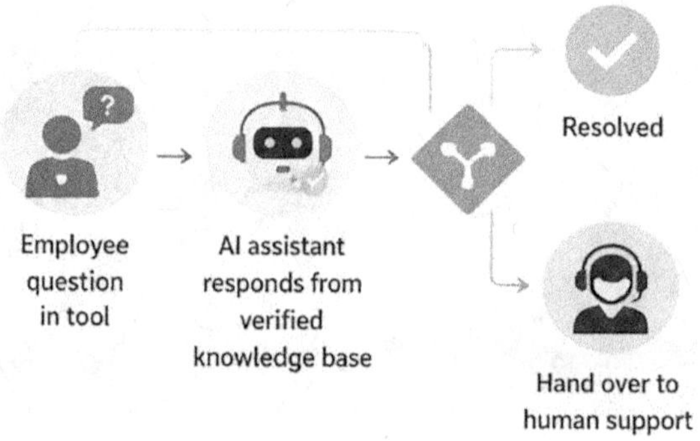

- Keep knowledge base current and tagged by topic.
- Track what people ask to spot gaps in training.
- Make it clear when and how to reach a human.

Designing a Useful Internal AI Assistant

Design decisions that make assistants useful

1. **Define scope clearly.**
Be explicit about what the assistant can answer and what it escalates. Set boundaries to avoid overreach.

2. **Build a curated knowledge base.**
Use trusted, up-to-date sources. Keep content owned, versioned, and easy to maintain.

3. **Write clear, Q&A-style content.**
Answer real questions in plain language. Use examples and link to single sources of truth.

4. **Design escalation pathways.**
Make it easy to hand off when needed. Provide "I don't know — here's who to ask."

5. **Monitor unanswered questions.**
Treat unknowns as signals of gaps in comms or training. Feed insights back to improve content.

What you Need to Remember

Start narrow and reliable.

Focus on the top questions that create the most impact. Keep answers accurate, evidence-based, and your content fresh with regular reviews.

Write for the assistant, not the policy manual.

Make answers crisp and complete. Use Q&A, examples, and links to single sources of truth.

Make gaps and escalations visible.

Build explicit handoffs and track unknowns. Feed them back into comms improvements and training.

1. Collect FAQs → 2. Draft Q&A content → 3. Build / connect knowledge base → 4. Define escalation owners → 5. Review unanswered questions

Quick setup checklist
- Named owner
- Single knowledge base
- Live escalation contacts

Success signals
- Fewer repeat questions
- Faster answers
- in channels

Keep improving
Review logs monthly, retire stale content, add new FAQs.

From Static FAQs to Adaptive Conversational Support

Shifting from Pages to Conversations

1. **Static FAQs are hard to find and don't cover everything.**
People waste time searching, clicking through pages, and still go unanswered.

2. **People ask questions in their own words.**
Conversations are natural, context-rich, and never one-size-fits-all.

3. **AI matches intent to the best answers.**
It understands meaning, handles variations, and delivers accurate replies.

4. **AI learns from every interaction and uncovers patterns.**
Usage data shows what people need, what's missing, and what to improve.

5. **Adaptive support drives better outcomes across the change.**
Insights feed the wider programme, helping teams plan, adjust, and succeed.

What you Need to Remember

Make help feel like a conversation, not a hunt through links.
People get fast, natural answers without leaving their flow of work.

Let AI handle messy questions and route to clear answers.
It understands intent, cuts the noise, and connects people to what matters.

Use question patterns as feedback to tune the whole change programme.
Better insights lead to smarter content, better experiences, and stronger results.

Ask in your own words → AI understands intent → Delivers answer & follow-ups → Insights improve change

Better conversations. Smarter insights. Stronger change.

Quick Checks for Your Support Channel

- Can people find answers without digging?
- Does it understand questions in their own words?
- Are we learning from what people are asking?

Signals It's Working

- More questions answered without human handoff
- Faster resolution and happier employees
- Insights driving content and programme improvements

Building a Role-Specific Messaging Framework

Designing Your Messaging Architecture

1 Map stakeholders and roles.
Capture who's affected, their influence, and how they experience the change.

2 Write one core change narrative
that explains the why, what will change, and what it means day to day.

3 Use AI to adapt the story
for each audience segment while keeping the same facts.

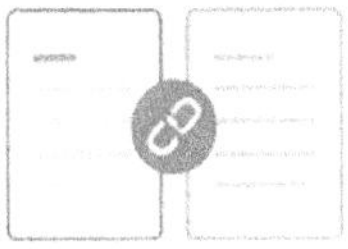

4 Lock a single source of truth.
Keep tone, key messages, and data points consistent across all variants.

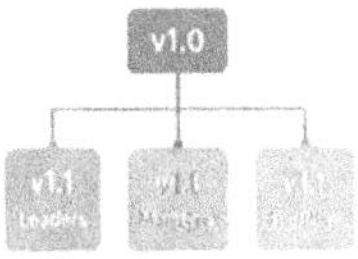

5 Version-control your drafts
so you can update the master narrative once and regenerate every role-specific message.

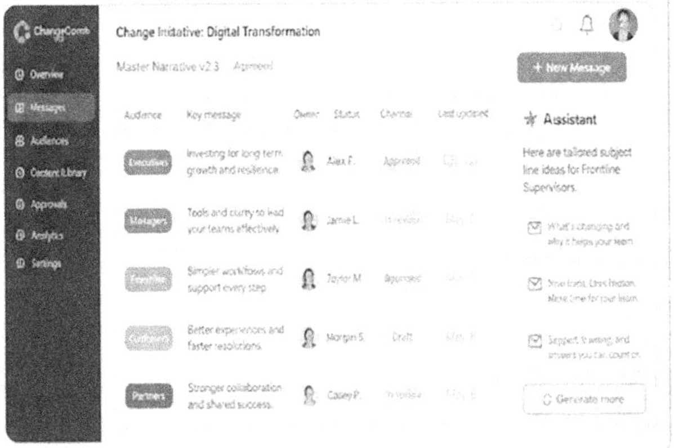

What you Need to Remember

Start with people, not tools.

Clarify roles, concerns, and impact before you ever prompt an AI. The architecture drives every message.

One narrative, many versions.

Keep a clear, approved change story and let AI localise tone, detail, and examples for each group.

Update the source, then regenerate.

When facts or decisions change, revise the master narrative and re-run your variants so everything stays aligned.

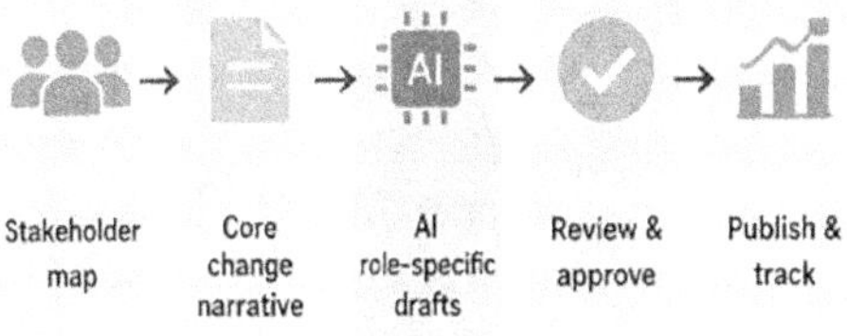

Quick prompts to try:

- 'Draft a role-specific update for frontline supervisors using this core narrative...'
- 'Turn this executive summary into an FAQ for customer-facing teams...'

Signals you're doing it well:

Messages match across channels, leaders reuse the same story, and updates reach every audience at the same time.

Practical Prompting for Change Communications

Designing Strong Prompts for Change Messages

1. **Set the scene clearly.** State role, change, key concerns, and desired tone in a sentence or two.
2. **Choose the output format.** Email, bullet brief, FAQ, or talk track — tell the AI exactly what to write.
3. **Explore variants.** Ask for 2–3 options to compare tone, length, and structure.
4. **Run a critique loop.** Have the AI highlight weaknesses in its own draft and suggest fixes.
5. **Turn winners into templates.** Save effective prompts for teammates and future changes.

What you Need to Remember

Context is your leverage.

The more you share about audience, change, and worries, the closer the first draft lands.

Format and tone shape impact.

Tell the AI how it should sound and where the message will be used.

Prompts are reusable assets.

Refine over time, store the best, and standardise great change communication.

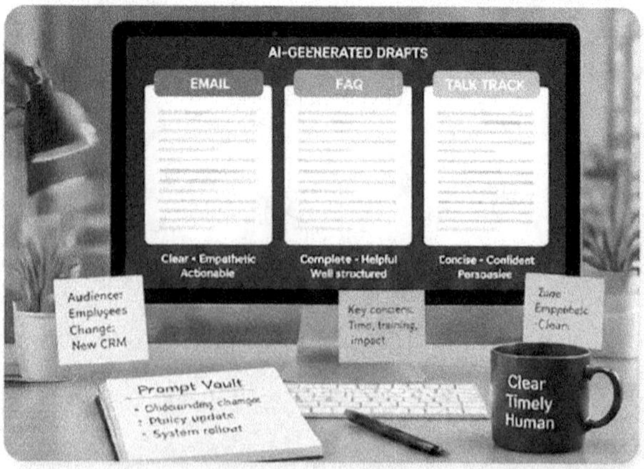

Context	Draft	Critique loop	Approved message
Who, what, why, concerns, and tone.	AI creates the first draft.	AI critiques its draft and proposes fixes.	Refined and ready to share.

Quick Starter Prompt

You are a communications specialist. Draft a [format] to explain [change] to [audience]. They're worried about [top concerns]. Use a [tone] tone and keep it to [length]. Then critique your own draft and suggest improvements.

- Copy and adapt for each change
- Store in your team playbook
- Review prompts after each major announcement.

AI-Supported Manager Toolkits

Building Better Manager Toolkits with AI

1

Managers are the primary voice in any change.

Their explanation shapes how people feel about the shift.

2

Most managers feel under-briefed and exposed.

They worry they can't answer questions or coach well.

3

Use AI to draft timely, role-specific support.

Generate toolkits that match team realities and current questions.

4

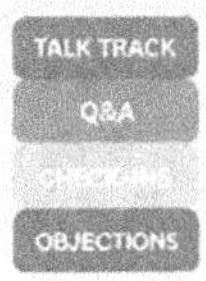

Standard toolkit pieces:

- Talk tracks for meetings
- Q&A guides
- Check-in prompts
- Objection handlers.

5

Co-create, don't just roll out.

Ask managers to review, adapt, and own the AI draft.

What you Need to
What you Need to Remember

Managers carry the change story.

Centre your toolkit on what they need to say, explain, and coach — not on head-office slides.

AI closes the confidence gap.

Use AI to turn high-level messages into concrete scripts, answers, and follow-up prompts for each manager type.

Involve managers early.

Pilot drafts with a small group, capture their edits, and bake their language into the final toolkit.

Listen to managers → Prompt the AI → Review & adapt together → Publish & update toolkit

Before launch: test toolkits in one real team meeting.

During rollout: track which questions managers still escalate.

Afterwards: schedule a quick AI refresh every quarter.

Designing Effective Manager Talk Tracks

Building a useful talk track

1. **Think aid, not script**
   Use prompts and structure to guide the conversation, not read it.
2. **Anchor to the purpose**
   Start with the why. Keep every point tied to the objective.
3. **Land 2–3 key messages**
   Focus on what matters most. Keep it clear, simple, and memorable.
4. **Anticipate likely questions**
   Identify what people may ask and prepare talking points in advance.
5. **Draft honest responses**
   Be transparent about what you know, what you don't, and what's next.

What you Need to Remember

Keep it conversational
Speak like a human. Use simple language and listen as much as you talk.

Invite real questions
Create space for honest questions. It builds trust and better decisions.

Always show the next step
People leave with clarity when you outline what happens next and who's responsible.

Brief & audience → **AI first draft** → **Manager edits for honesty** → **Agree escalation path**

- **Brief & audience**: Understand the situation and who you're talking to.
- **AI first draft**: Let AI build a strong starting version.
- **Manager edits for honesty**: Add context, tone, and your true point of view.
- **Agree escalation path**: Confirm when and how to escalate issues.

Before the meeting

- Know the purpose.
- Review key facts and updates.
- Check your talk track.
- Prepare for likely questions.

During the conversation

- Open with the purpose.
- Share key messages clearly.
- Listen actively.
- Invite questions and respond.
- Summarize and set next step.

After the conversation

- Document key takeaways.
- Share actions and owners.
- Follow up on commitments.
- Update your talk track.

Keeping Toolkits Current and Contextual

Keeping Toolkits Alive

1. **Change keeps moving**
   Work, risks, and priorities shift—toolkits must keep up.
2. **Update fast with AI**
   Use AI to refresh content, rewrite, and tailor to context.
3. **Version every release**
   Every update gets a version, owner, and publish date.
4. **Flag what's changed**
   Make updates easy to spot so people know what's new.
5. **Support with live Q&A**
   Give people a fast way to get answers on real-world cases.

What you Need to Remember

Out-of-date toolkits erode trust – treat them as living products.

Use AI + light governance: small, frequent releases with clear owners and dates.

Help managers focus: highlight what's new and offer an AI Q&A channel for edge cases.

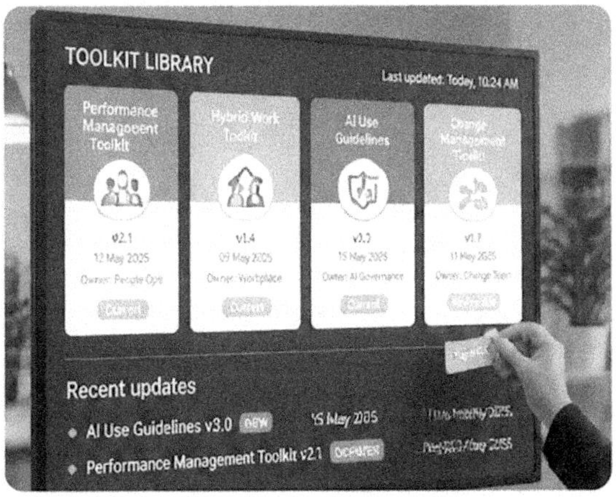

- Set a review cadence (e.g., fortnightly).
- Archive old versions, don't delete.
- Track questions to spot gaps in the toolkit.

AI-Generated Learning Content

Using AI to Build Learning Faster

1. Traditional training is slow; AI speeds up the whole content lifecycle.
2. AI is ideal for short microlearning at point of need.
3. AI can draft guides, checklists, scenarios, quizzes, practice prompts.
4. Instructional design still needed – humans set goals, sequence, measures.
5. Output quality depends on the source knowledge you give the AI.

What you Need to Remember

AI accelerates production, not design.

Humans decide what learners must do, design the pathway, and then use AI to draft materials quickly.

Keep it small and practical.

Favour bite-sized, task-focused modules people can use immediately, instead of long courses.

Feed AI with real expertise.

Provide accurate source material and local context, then review, adapt, and test content with real users.

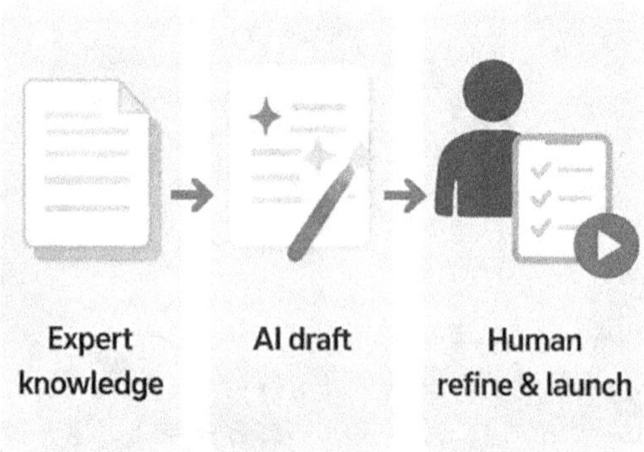

When you use AI for learning, remember to:

- Clarify the learning outcome first
- Protect confidential data
- Pilot with a small group before scaling

Types of AI-Generated Learning Content

AI Learning Content Types

1) Step-by-step process guides

Short, numbered walkthroughs for new tools or workflows.

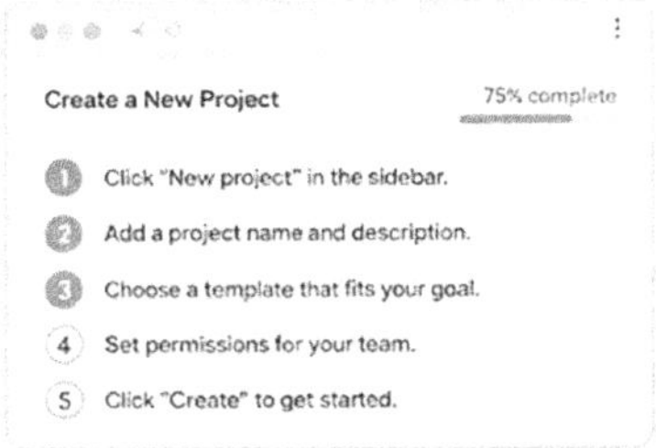

2) Scenario-based learning

Realistic situations that force a decision and show consequences.

3) Knowledge checks & quizzes

Micro-quizzes before and after to confirm understanding.

4) Practice prompts

Ready-made prompts learners can test in their own environment.

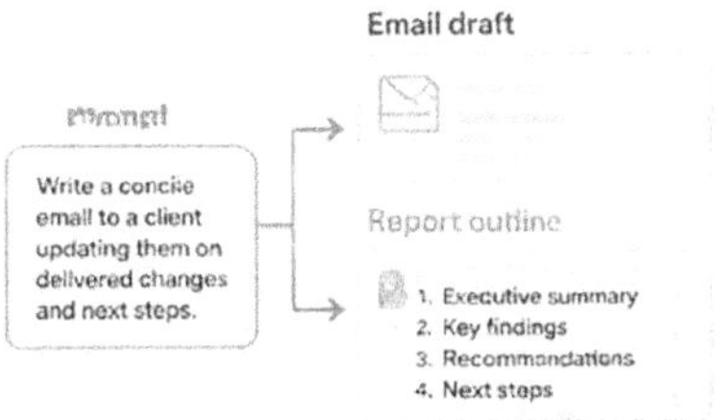

5) Simulated dialogues

Model conversations for coaching and communication skills.

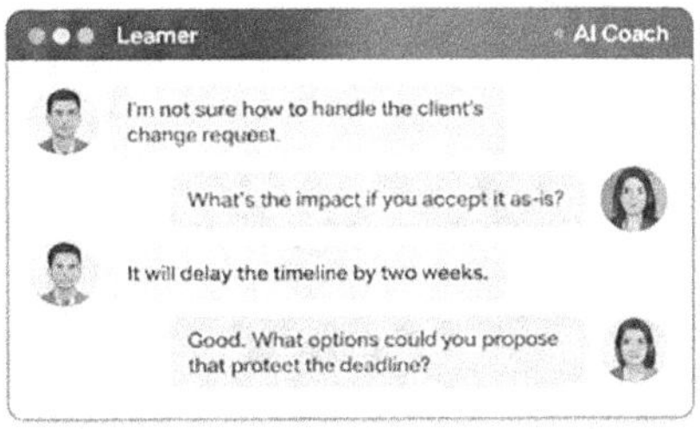

What you Need to Remember

1. Mix formats for deeper learning.

Combine guides, scenarios, quizzes, and prompts so learners see, try, and check their understanding in one flow.

2. Make it realistic and immediately usable.

Use real tasks, tools, and decisions learners face this week, not abstract examples.

3. Turn AI from demo to practice.

End every module with prompts or dialogues people can copy, adapt, and try straight away.

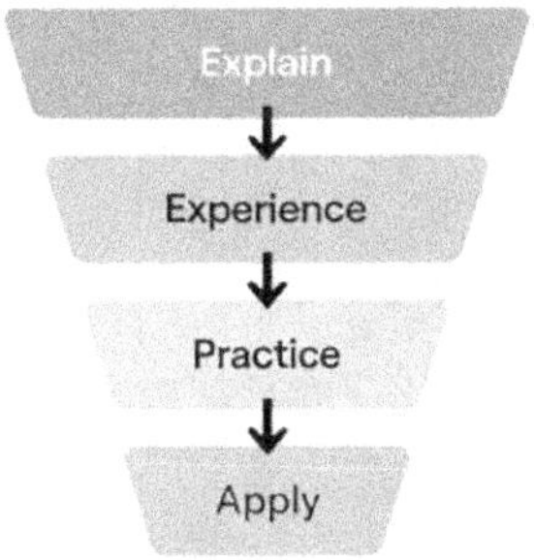

When designing with AI, ask:

- What problem should this content solve?
- Which format helps people act differently?
- Where will learners try this in real work?

Pick task → Choose format → Generate with AI → Test with learners

Quality Control for AI-Generated Learning

Quality checks before content goes live

1. **Verify facts, especially technical, policy, and procedural details.**
   Cross-check with source documents or a subject-matter expert.
2. **Check scenarios against real work.**
   Names, systems, and workflows should match how people actually work.
3. **Pilot with a small group.**
   Ask: "Does this reflect how we really do things?" Capture feedback before launch.
4. **Ensure accessibility.**
   Plain language, readable structure, inclusive visuals, and captions where needed.
5. **Apply a review gate.**
   No module goes live without a named reviewer signing it off.

What you Need to Remember

Speed doesn't replace review.
Use AI to draft fast, then slow down for checking, piloting, and sign-off.

Real context builds trust.
Learners engage when scenarios look and feel like their own work.

Accessibility is non-negotiable.
Design so everyone can participate, not just the average user.

MINIMAL QC WORKFLOW

1. AI draft
2. Expert check
3. Pilot & refine
4. Final sign-off

Source checked? | Real users reviewed? | Accessibility tested?

Measuring Behaviour Change with AI

Seeing Real Adoption, Not Just Awareness

1. Adoption = repeated behaviour, not just knowing the change exists.
2. Use AI to read usage across tools, journeys, and roles, not one system at a time.
3. Treat errors, workarounds, and drop-offs as gold: they show where change is failing.
4. Let AI flag weak points early so you can coach, simplify, or redesign before habits set.
5. Measure continuously so you see trends, not just a single post-rollout score.

What you Need to Remember

Look for behaviour, not noise.
Pair comms metrics with real usage: log-ins, task completion, and who reverts to old tools.

Treat friction as a signal to help.
Spikes in errors or workarounds mean 'fix the flow', not 'push harder'. Change the process, training, or tooling.

Keep the change on a live feed.
Use AI dashboards and alerts so leaders see progress weekly and can step in before momentum drops.

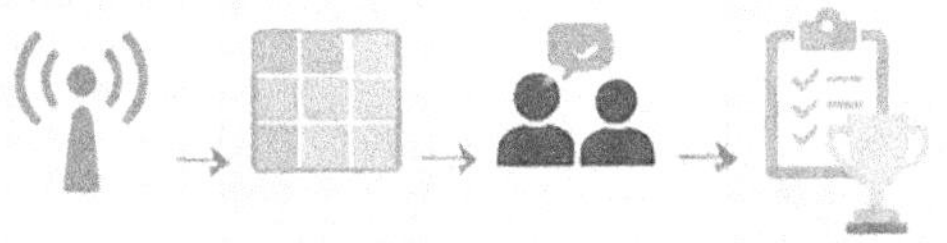

AI collects signals	Spot friction hotspots	Targeted support	New stable habits
Usage, events, errors, and behaviour data.	AI surfaces where people get stuck or drop off.	Provide coaching, resources, or tools to remove friction.	Better flows and confidence create lasting change.

Quick Checks for Change Leads

- Can I see where people are reverting to old ways?
- Do we act on AI insights within days, not months?
- Are we tracking adoption by team, not just overall?

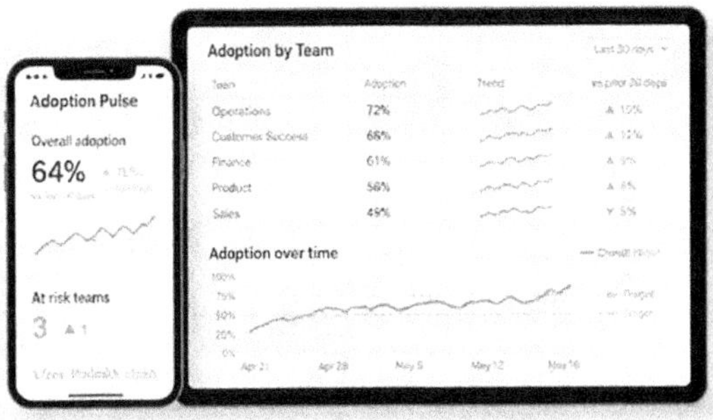

Adoption Dashboards and Narrative Reporting

Building an Adoption Dashboard

1. **Combine usage, sentiment, milestones.**
   Blend quantitative, qualitative, and progress data for a complete picture.

2. **Show trends, not just snapshots.**
   Track change over time to see momentum and impact.

3. **Slice by team, role, region.**
   Filter and compare to find what's working — and where.

4. **Flag risk and wins visually.**
   Use clear signals to surface issues and celebrate progress.

5. **End with a clear "focus next" call-out.**
   Make the next best action obvious for your audience.

What you Need to Remember

Data + story drives action.
Leaders need meaning, not spreadsheets — connect insights to decisions.

Segment to target support.
Find lagging teams and tailor help to their needs and context.

Every report answers: Where next?
Give your reader one clear priority so they know what to do.

Using AI for Narrative Reporting

- Turn metrics into plain language summaries.
- Explain what's changing and why it matters.
- Highlight risks, wins, and next steps.

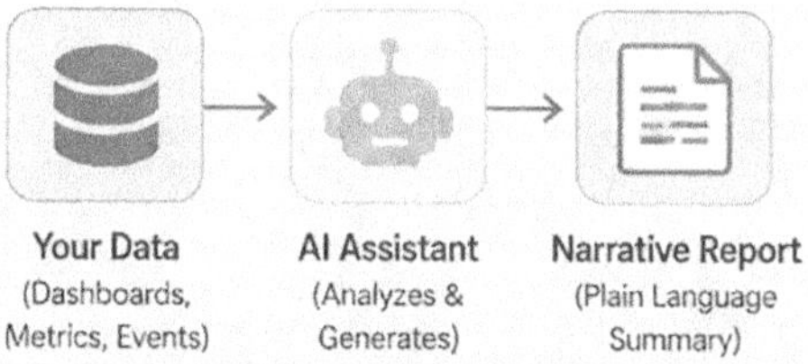

> "Engagement is trending up, led by Marketing and Sales. Finance usage is low — investigate workflow friction. Overall sentiment improved, driven by faster onboarding.
>
> Focus Next: Drive Finance onboarding and simplify key workflows.

Checklist before sharing a dashboard

1. **Clear question** — Is the purpose and audience clear?
2. **Key segments** — Have you shown the right slices?
3. **One call to action** — Is the "focus next" obvious?

Continuous Improvement Loops

How AI Tightens the Loop

1. **Assume iteration**
   Every launch is version 1. We improve with every cycle.
2. **Listen at scale**
   AI scans feedback channels across teams, tools, and touchpoints.
3. **Spot patterns fast**
   AI themes issues and wins so we focus on what matters most.
4. **Feed insights into action**
   Update comms, training, and manager nudges based on what we learn.
5. **Shorten the lag**
   Move from feedback to impact in days, not weeks.

What you Need to Remember

Design for learning, not perfection.

No model or plan is perfect. Build safe loops so we can learn fast and get better every cycle.

Use AI to hear every voice.

AI helps us capture and understand feedback from across the organisation—not just the loudest ones.

Act visibly on what you learn.

People engage when they see their feedback leads to real changes.
Show the loop. Earn trust. Drive results.

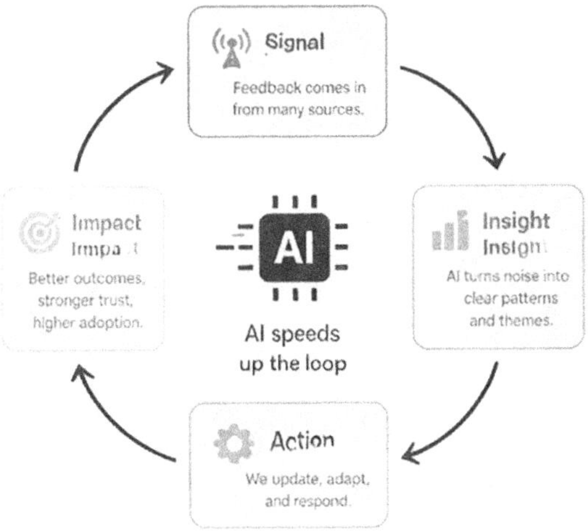

Quick prompts for your team

- What are we hearing that we didn't expect?
- What's one thing we can improve this week?
- Who needs to see this insight?

Signals your loop is working

- Faster response to feedback.
- More people sharing feedback.
- Visible improvements drive engagement.

Value Realisation and Benefits Tracking

Linking Adoption to Business Value

1. **Connect adoption to outcomes**
   Usage is only useful when tied to productivity, quality, or cost.
2. **Use AI to join up data**
   Combine behavioural data with performance metrics automatically.
3. **Track benefits continuously**
   Move from one-off reviews to a live benefits dashboard.
4. **Translate into ROI language**
   Frame improvements as time saved, errors reduced, and value created.
5. **Build credibility for the next change**
   Clear value stories make sponsorship easier next time.

What you Need to Remember

Always link behaviour to outcomes.
If you can't show impact on productivity, quality, or efficiency, the metric won't land.

Make value visible in real time.
Use AI-driven dashboards so sponsors can see benefits as they appear, not a year later.

Use results to earn trust for future change.
Share simple before-and-after stories that prove change delivers.

Capture adoption data → Link to performance KPIs → Quantify financial impact → Share value story

Questions to ask

- What outcome are we trying to move?
- Do we have the data to prove it?
- Who needs to see this value story?

Fast signals of success

- Leaders quote value numbers
- Teams ask for more analytics, not less
- Benefits dashboard used in exec meetings

Avoid

- Tracking usage with no link to outcomes
- Presenting benefits only once, long after go-live.

SECTION 4

Functional and Sector Use Cases

This section grounds the earlier methods in concrete functional and sector settings. It opens with enterprise change in Microsoft 365 environments, showing how to use Copilot where people already work, with Word for policy, communications, and leadership messaging, Excel for analysis and reporting, PowerPoint for mobilisation and storytelling, and Copilot agents built for business users. It then turns to cross-platform knowledge work with ChatGPT and Claude, using ChatGPT for rapid synthesis and action-oriented workflows, Claude for long documents and structured reasoning, comparing outputs across tools, and building a multi-tool operating model.

The section then explores sector-specific change scenarios, tailoring AI-enabled change to context and drawing out the characteristic patterns in financial services and regulated transformation, healthcare and public services, manufacturing and operations, and professional services and knowledge firms.

It closes with role-based adoption pathways, setting out what adoption looks like for executives and sponsors, change managers and PMO teams, people managers and team leaders, and end users and specialists. The point is that the same underlying techniques land differently depending on the tool environment, the sector's constraints, and the role of the person adopting them.

By the end you should be able to match AI-enabled change approaches to your own platform mix, industry, and audience, rather than applying a single template everywhere. The section turns general capability into targeted practice, helping change leaders see exactly where and how AI fits the situation in front of them.

Using Copilot Where People Already Work

Copilot inside everyday M365 apps

1 Word

Copilot is built into Word.

2 Excel

Copilot is built into Excel.

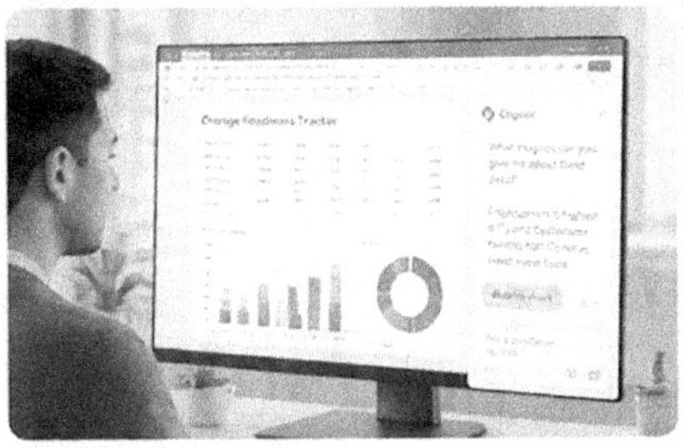

3 PowerPoint

Copilot is built into PowerPoint.

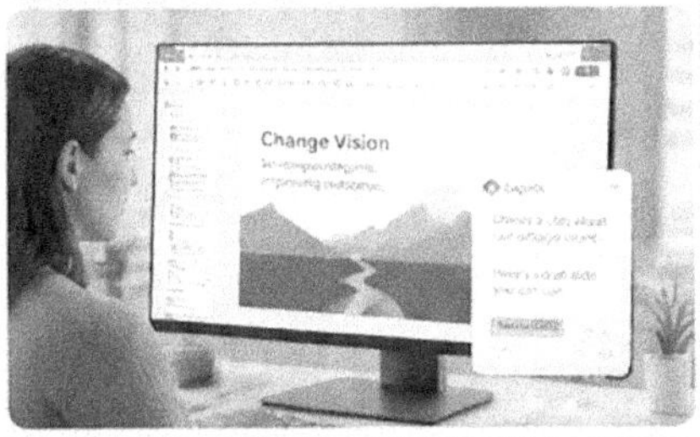

4 Teams & Outlook

Copilot is built into Teams and Outlook.

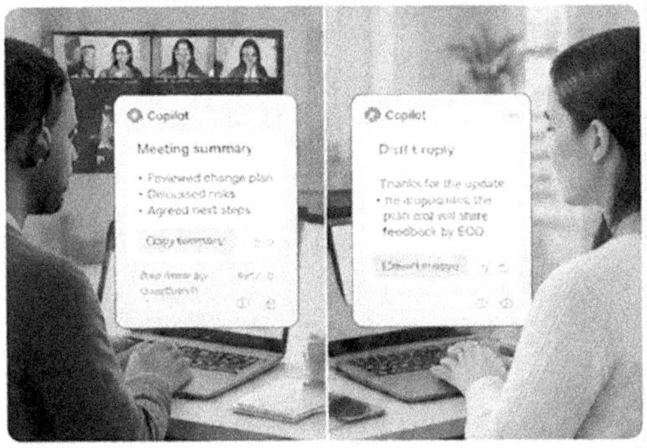

What you Need to Remember

Reuse the tools people already know

Lower friction by keeping change work in Word, Excel, PowerPoint, Teams, and Outlook.

Lead by example in the same workspace

Show your own Copilot use live in documents, meetings, and emails.

Focus on high-impact Copilot surfaces

Prioritise scenarios where AI removes busywork for change leaders and teams.

Next steps for change leaders

- Identify one change task to tackle this week.
- Try Copilot in the app you already use.
- Share what you learned and encourage others.

Pick a change task → Try it with Copilot → Share what you learned

Word for Policy, Comms, and Leadership Messaging

Using Copilot in Word for Change Writing

1 Change writing workload is heavy

Policies, comms, and updates demand clear, consistent words—fast.

Your document backlog
- Policy update.docx
- Leadership note.docx
- Comms brief.docx
- FAQ update.docx
- Stakeholder letter.pdf

2 Copilot drafts, reformats, and summarises

Turn a rough brief into structured, ready-to-use content in seconds.

File Home Insert Draw Design Layout References
Copilot

Original brief (rough): We need to tell staff about the policy changes. Make it clear and keep it short.
→
Copilot rewrite: We're updating our policy to make work simpler and fairer. Here's what's changing and what you need to know.

3 Adjust tone for each audience

Make it formal, plain, confident, or empathetic—as needed.

Choose a tone: Formal | Plain | Confident | Empathetic

Preview: We are introducing changes to improve clarity and support for all teams.

4 You own the judgement

You know the context, stakeholders, and risks—always review and approve.

Before you approve
- ✓ Does it fit the audience?
- ✓ Is the content accurate?
- ✓ Any policy or legal risks?
- ✓ Is the tone right?

5 Tighten version control

Track changes, name clearly, and share the right version.

v1.0 – v1.1 – v2.0

Change Comms – Versions
- Change Comms_v1.0.docx — 2 May
- Change Comms_v1.1.docx — 6 May
- Change Comms_v2.0 (final).docx — 12 May ✓

What you Need to Remember

Start with a clear prompt
State your goal, audience, and tone so Copilot can write with purpose.

Use Copilot to tailor, not to decide
Review for fit, accuracy, and risk—then make the call.

Control your drafts
Name, save, and share the current version—no guesswork.

Your 4-step workflow

Prompt → **Draft** → **Review** → **Send**

- **Prompt:** Give Copilot clear context and goals.
- **Draft:** Copilot creates content in seconds.
- **Review:** Check for fit, accuracy, and risk.
- **Send:** Approve and share with confidence.

Great outputs start with clear prompts and end with human judgement.

Good prompts to try
- "Turn this briefing into a leadership email."
- "Create a team update in plain English."
- "Rewrite this policy summary for a busy exec."

Checks before sending
- Facts accurate?
- Tone and audience right?
- Any risks or sensitive information?

When to *not* rely on Copilot
Don't rely on Copilot for confidential, legally sensitive, or high-risk content—always use expert judgement.

Excel for Analysis and Reporting

Using Copilot with Change Data

1 Most change data lives in Excel
readiness scores, surveys, training, benefits trackers

Date	Department	Readiness Score	Training %	Survey Score	Benefits Realized
6 May	Finance	72	85%	4.1	$125,000
6 May	HR	48	62%	3.2	$ 78,000
6 May	IT	83	91%	4.6	$210,000
6 May	Operations	56	67%	3.4	$ 95,000
6 May	Sales	61	73%	3.7	$110,000

2 Ask questions in plain language
e.g. 'Which teams have lowest readiness?

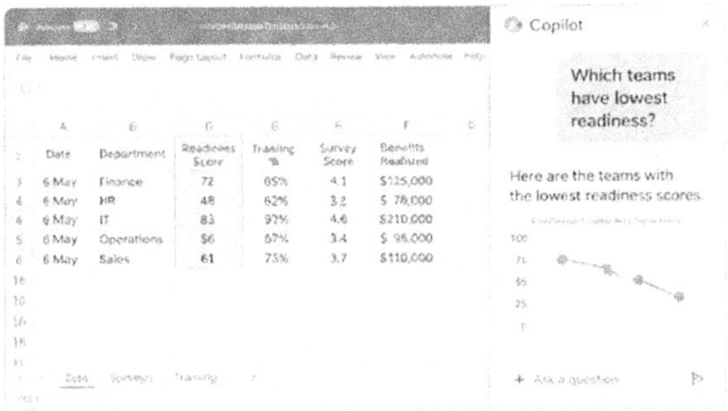

3 Generate formulas and charts automatically
lower barrier for non-specialists

fx =AVERAGEIF(B2:B6,"Finance",C2:C6)

4 Build lightweight adoption dashboards
slice by department, time period, activity

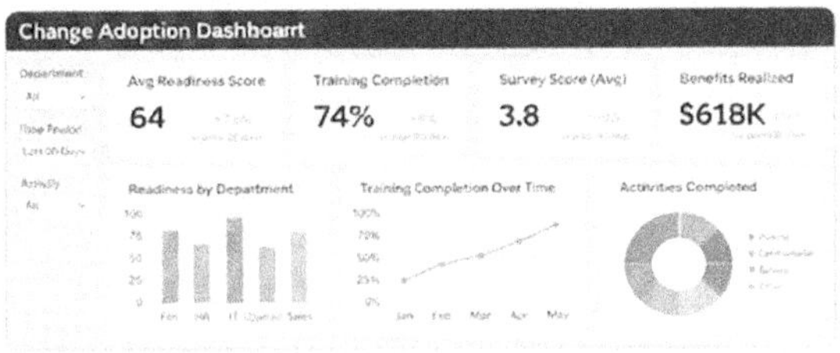

5 Validate before you share
check logic, data ranges, and assumptions

- Check formula logic and results
- Confirne ranges and filters
- Review assumptions and definitions
- Spot outliers and data quality issues

Quick checks before sharing:

- Is the source data clean?
- Do the visuals match the message?
- Would I stand by this in a leadership meeting?

What you Need to Remeember

Let Copilot do the heavy lifting

Use it to explore data, surface trends, and draft charts fast.

Stay in control of the story

Decide which findings matter, add context, and link to change outcomes.

Trust, but verify

Treat outputs as a first draft.
Re-run checks and sense-check before presenting to leaders.

PowerPoint for Mobilisation and Storytelling

Using Copilot in PowerPoint

1. **Change work = constant decks.**
Executive updates, training, launches, and progress reviews always need slides.

2. **Prompt to build the first draft.**
Ask Copilot to create a short deck from a plain-language prompt or change brief.

3. **Turn docs into narratives.**
Upload strategy or impact documents and let Copilot structure them into a storyline.

4. **Refine for each audience.**
Use Copilot to summarise long decks, add speaker notes, and reframe for different groups.

5. **AI structure, human polish.**
You keep control of message, visuals, and alignment to brand standards.

What you Need to Remember

Start from the messy source.
Feed Copilot your change strategy docs, meeting notes, or draft emails to jump-start the deck.

Use AI to move faster, not skip thinking.
Check every slide for clarity, risks, and stakeholder impact. Edit examples and visuals so they feel real for your organisation.

Make the story for humans in the room.
Tailor language, time, and visuals for execs, frontline staff, or partners so each group sees 'what this means for me.'

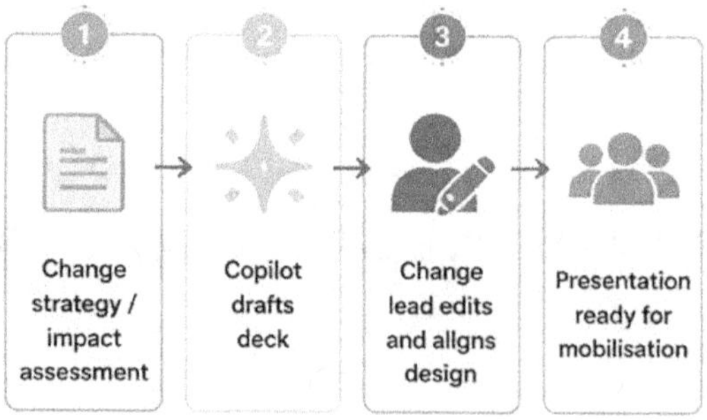

Quick Checks Before You Present

- [x] Is the storyline simple and outcome-focused?
- [x] Do slides show 'before vs after' for this change?
- [x] Have you removed jargon and unused slides?

Copilot Agents for Business Users

How Copilot Agents Help

1 Go beyond one-off prompts

Agents handle multi-step, goal-based tasks from start to finish—so you get outcomes, not just answers.

2 Work inside Teams & Copilot Chat

Talk to agents in the Microsoft 365 apps you already use—no new tools or switching context.

3 Use your organisation's data

Connect to SharePoint, knowledge bases, databases, and line-of-business systems so agents answer with trusted, up-to-date information.

4 Solve real business needs

Onboarding assistant
Help new hires get up to speed fast.

Policy Q&A
Find answers to policies, procedures, and FAQs.

Adoption support channel
Provide guidance and tips right when people need it.

5 Build in Copilot Studio

Use low-code tools to design, test, and publish agents—no developer skills required.

What you Need to Remember

Think in workflows, not prompts
Agents are designed to plan, take action, and deliver results—across multiple steps and systems.

Connect to the right data
Great answers come from trusted, governed sources. Use the right content, permissions, and freshness to ensure accuracy.

Empower change managers to build
Change managers know the business and the users. With Copilot Studio, they can build agents that drive adoption and impact.

How it works

Employees ask
Questions and requests in natural language

↓

Copilot Agent
Plans, takes action, and reasons over your data

↓

Answers from your content
Accurate, relevant, and secure responses

Clarify the goal
Define the outcome you want the agent to achieve.

Decide which content the agent can use
Choose sources, set permissions, and keep content up to date.

Pilot with a small group and iterate
Learn, refine, and scale based on real feedback.

ChatGPT for Rapid Synthesis and Action-Oriented Workflows

Using ChatGPT as a Momentum Engine

1. Turn rough briefs into usable drafts fast – emails, decks, plans, talking points.

2. Pulls from multiple sources and produces a clear, coherent synthesis or recommendation.

3. With web browsing and tools, handle 'research-to-output' tasks in one place.

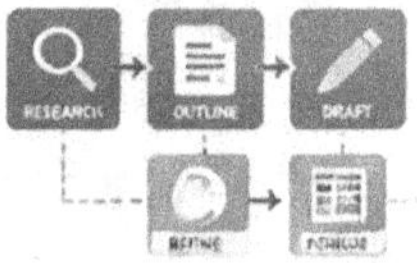

4. Agent-style workflows chain steps: research → outline → draft → refine → format.

5. Best for speed, breadth and momentum – not forensic accuracy or policy decisions.

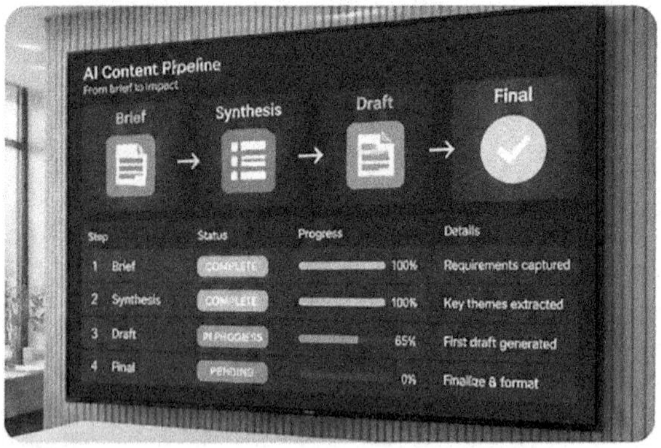

What you Need to Remember

Use ChatGPT to keep work moving.

Treat it as a momentum tool: get from idea to first draft in a single pass, then edit.

Aim for landscape, not microscope.

Ask for overviews, options and recommendations rather than perfect detail.

Design end-to-end workflows.

Combine browsing, tools and agents so ChatGPT completes a whole task, not just a reply.

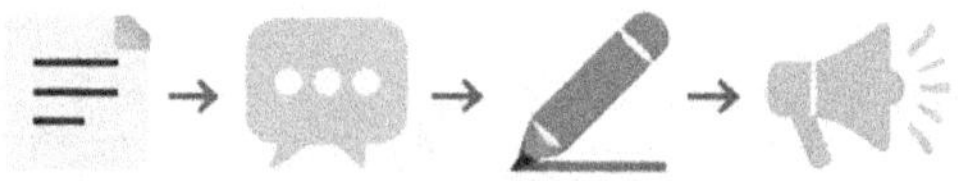

Rough brief → **ChatGPT draft** → **Human edit** → **Share & act**

Quick prompts to try:

- "Turn this messy meeting note into a concise action plan."
- "Scan these links and summarise key themes for leaders."
- "Design a 3-step workflow so this task takes less time next week."

Claude for Long Documents and Structured Reasoning

Using Claude for Deep, Structured Work

1. **Keep whole policies or contracts in view**
   Work with the full document so nothing important is missed.
2. **Ask for step-by-step reasoning, not just answers**
   Structure the thinking so you can follow every step.
3. **Use Claude to draft precise, defensible text**
   Get clear, well-structured language you can stand behind.
4. **Let Claude do impact analysis; you decide what matters**
   See the ripple effects so you can prioritize with confidence.
5. **Maintain control and oversight**
   You set the boundaries. Claude supports your decisions.

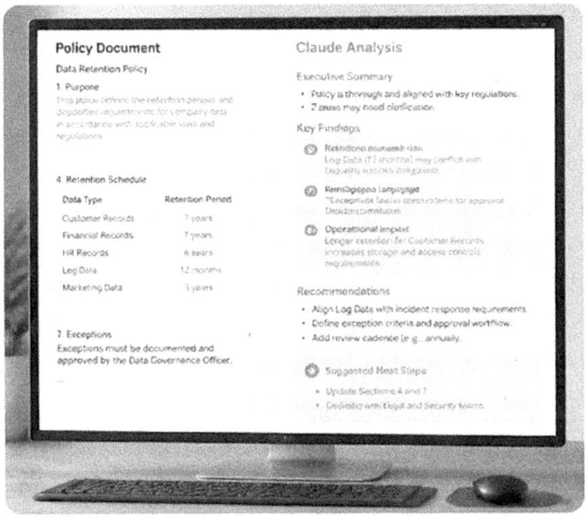

What you Need to Remember

1. **Depth over speed**
   Claude excels at understanding and reasoning through long, complex documents when given the time and context it needs.
2. **Controlled, defensible outputs**
   Guide Claude to produce outputs in the right tone and structure, with clear sources and audit trails you can trust.
3. **Use when stakes are high**
   Apply Claude to high-stakes work like policy, contracts, and sensitive content where accuracy and accountability matter.

Upload / paste document → Set structure & questions → Let Claude reason step-by-step → Review, edit, and sign off

Good prompts for Claude

- Walk through this policy section by section
- Highlight any ambiguous clauses
- Explain risks and suggested fixes

When NOT to use Claude alone

- Final legal sign-off
- Decisions without human review

Quick workflow tip

Save successful prompt templates and reuse them to keep quality high and speed up future work.

Comparing Outputs across Tools

How the Tools Differ

1. **Same prompt, different style**
   Expect meaningfully different outputs from ChatGPT and Claude.
2. **ChatGPT: bold & action-oriented**
   Great for drafts that need energy, options, and clear next steps.
3. **Claude: measured & structured**
   Suited to formal, cautious, or complex explanations.
4. **Governance & risk fit**
   In regulated work, prefer precise, auditable language.
5. **Build comparison judgement**
   Compare outputs to decide which tool to trust for each task.

What you Need to Remember

1. **Always compare at least two tools.**
   Run the same prompt and scan for tone, risk, and clarity.
2. **Match tool to context.**
   Use bolder outputs for comms and ideation; use measured language for policy, risk, and sensitive topics.
3. **Check governance and defensibility.**
   Ask: Would I be comfortable explaining this wording to an auditor or senior leader?

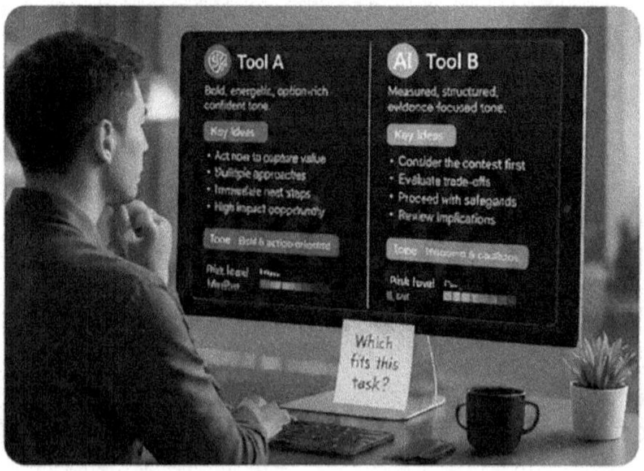

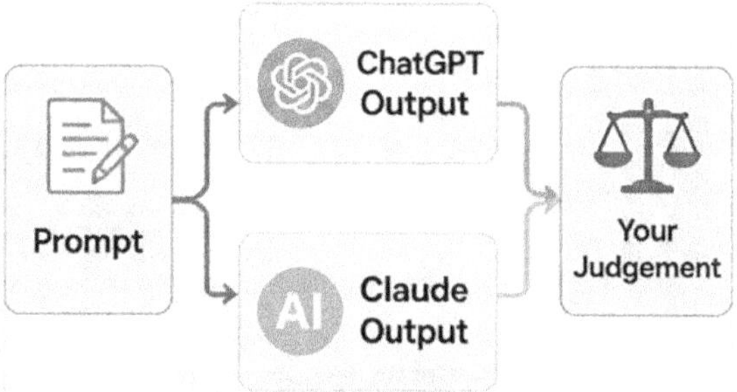

- Scan for over-confident claims.
- Note where language feels cautious vs bold.
- Capture which tool you'd re-use and why.

Building a Multi-Tool Operating Model

Designing your multi-tool model

1. Unplanned switching creates inconsistent quality and governance gaps
2. Define which tools are used for which task types
3. Use shared decision rules – don't let everyone choose differently each time
4. Select tools by task type, sensitivity, precision, workflow stage
5. Aim for deliberate, consistent, auditable AI use across the change team.

What you Need to Remember

Make tool choice a team rule.

When everyone follows the same rules, we get better outcomes, safer use, and fewer surprises.

Match tool to task risk.

Higher risk needs higher control. Use the right tool for the stakes of the work.

Keep the model visible and evolving.

Make it easy to see, update, and learn from how we use tools so the model gets better over time.

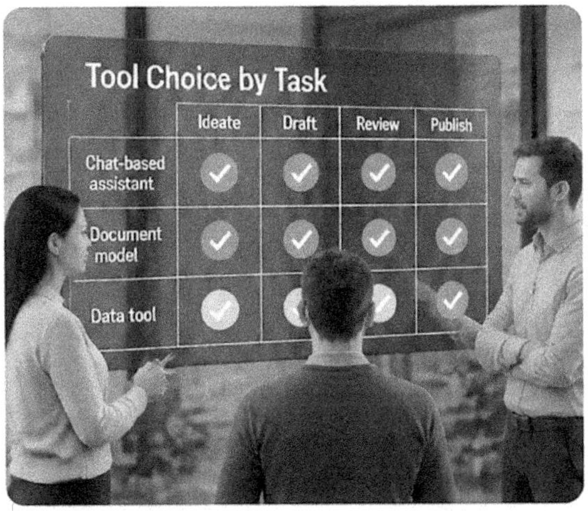

Map tasks → Set tool rules → Apply & log use → Review & refine

- Checklist before you start a task
- Where to log tool choices
- Who owns updates to the model

Tailoring AI-Enabled Change to Context

Reading the Context

1 Context drives AI change.
Sector economics, mission, and maturity set the boundaries.

2 Regulation sets the guardrails.
Data rules, audit duties, liability shape how fast you move.

3 Workforce profile matters.
Skills, unions, digital confidence affect adoption tactics.

4 Risk culture decides appetite.
Tolerance for failure, safety expectations drive pilots vs. big-bang.

5 Same tool, different playbook.
Expect variation; design per sector, not per product.

What you Need to Remember

Start with sector realities.
Before choosing tools, map regulation, workforce, data sensitivity, and risk norms.

Adapt, don't copy-paste.
Reuse frameworks, but tune language, pilots, and governance to each environment.

Design for what will land.
Pick use cases, training, and metrics that solve visible pain in that sector.

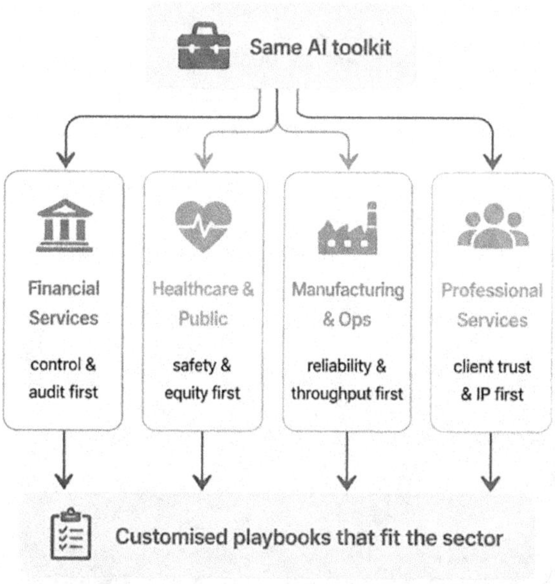

Quick Sector Scan Before You Act

- Regulation & data?
- Who will be most affected?
- What could go wrong here?

If you can answer these, you're ready to design change

- Why this sector needs AI now
- Where early wins are safest
- Who owns ongoing governance

Financial Services and Regulated Transformation

Designing AI Change in Financial Services

1. **Start with governance, not tools**
   Approvals, data classification, audit needs define AI design.
2. **Build human review into risky use cases**
   Client-facing or risk decisions must be checked and traceable.
3. **Respect the compliance message**
   AI drafts must match approved tone and wording.
4. **Map the stakeholder web**
   Front office, risk, legal, compliance, ops each own different risks.
5. **Use AI inside documented frameworks**
   Only deploy where roles, data and controls are defined.

What you Need to Remember

Governance is the product

Treat approvals, audit trails, and controls as part of the AI solution, not overhead.

Human eyes on high-stakes outputs

Anything influencing clients, capital, or conduct risk needs review, attribution, and a retrievable record.

Orchestrate the stakeholders

Align front office, risk, legal, compliance, and operations on where AI fits and who is accountable.

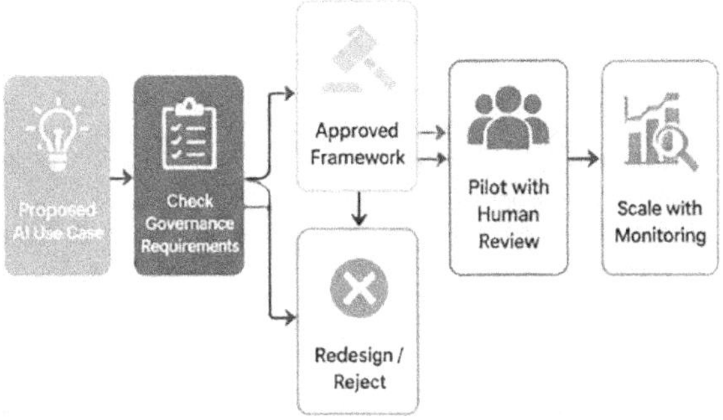

Quick Checks

- Can we show who approved this AI use?
- Is every risky output reviewable by a human?

Signals You're in Good Shape

- Issues caught in review, not by regulators.
- Stakeholders can explain the AI governance in plain language.

If in Doubt

Pause the workflow and escalate to risk or compliance.

Key AI Change Patterns in Financial Services

Using AI in Regulated Change Work

1. **Draft change impact** assessments aligned to regulation — AI creates first cut, humans refine.
2. **Generate first-draft** compliance messages only; legal, risk and comms own final wording.
3. **Run sentiment analysis** on pulse surveys to spot adoption friction early and target support.
4. **Offer AI-assisted FAQs** so staff can query new procedures and get consistent, approved answers.
5. **Capture prompts, inputs,** outputs and reviewers as part of the change audit trail.

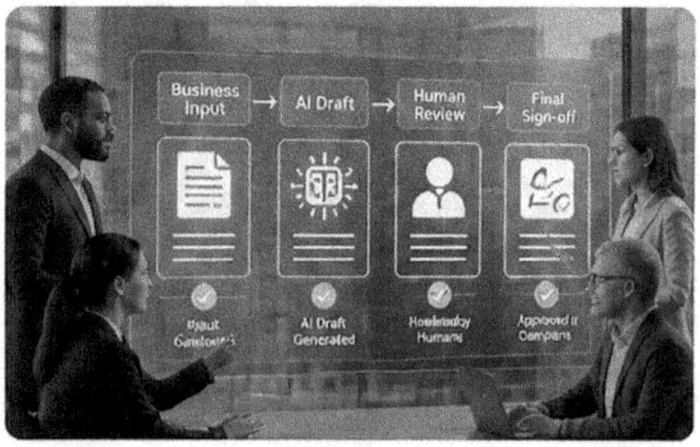

Quick checks for change leaders

- Is AI only drafting, not approving?
- Do reviewers know they are accountable?
- Is every AI-supported step logged?

What you Need to Remember

AI speeds drafting, not accountability.

Treat AI as a fast analyst. Policies, sign-off and liability stay with humans.

Use AI to sense tension early.

Mine comments and survey data so you can intervene before adoption drops.

Govern every interaction.

Standard prompts, approved training data, and full logs keep regulators comfortable.

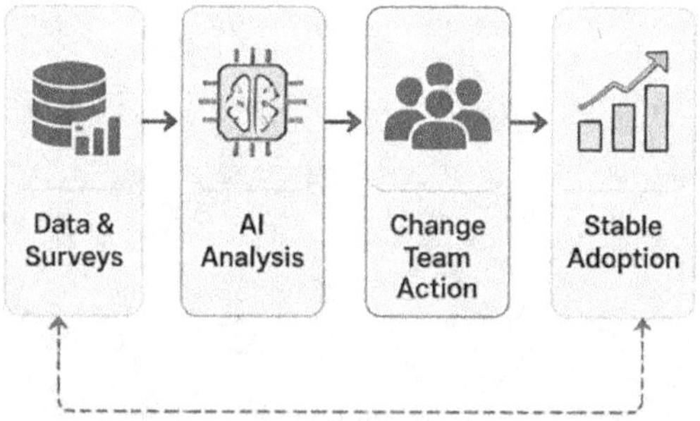

- **Design:** define which change artefacts AI can draft.
- **Controls:** agree review steps with Risk, Legal, Compliance.
- **Evidence:** keep examples of AI-supported decisions for regulators.

Healthcare and Public Services

Designing AI for pressured frontilne teams

1 Acknowledge pressure, fatigue, and change saturati

Frontline teams are stretched. Design AI that reduces friction, not adds to it.

2 Keep messages short, plain-language, and channel-appropriate.

Use clear words and the right channel at the right time.

3 Offer different AI onboarding paths for different skill levels.

Meet people where they are so everyone can succeed.

4 Explain clearly what AI does and where humans stay in charge.

Build trust by being open about roles, limits, and decisions.

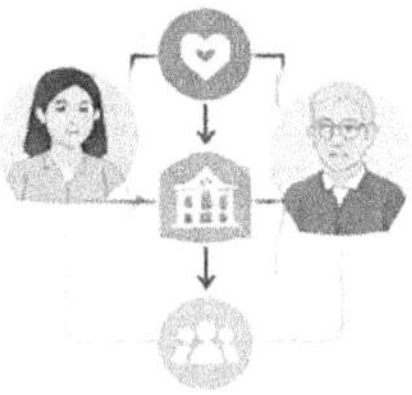

5 Track patient and citizen impact in every redesign scenario.

Measure what matters and use feedback to keep improving.

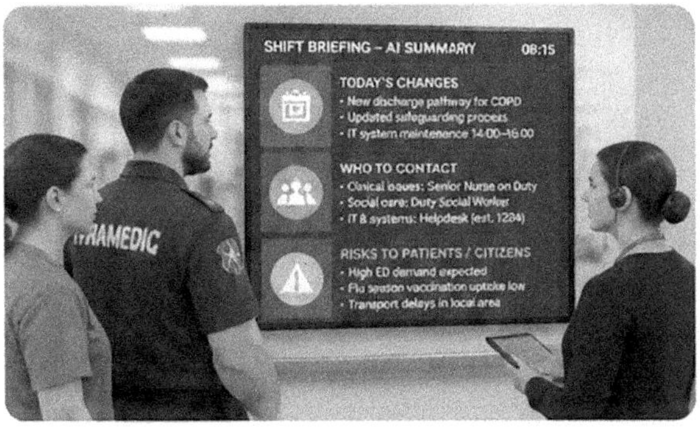

What you Need to Remember

Start with empathy for staff pressure.

Recognise workload and fatigue before you ask people to change how they work.

Communicate in fast, role-specific bites.

Design AI messages that can be understood in seconds, not minutes.

Be transparent with the public and protect outcomes.

Explain clearly how AI is used, where humans decide, and how you're monitoring impact on patients and citizens.

AI-enabled service redesign

1. Understand work on the ground
2. Co-design with staff & citizens
3. Decide what AI supports
4. Monitor results & adjust

Good prompts to generate briefings

- Summarise this policy for paramedics on night shift.
- List key changes for social workers today.
- Draft a 60-second update for call centre staff.

Signals you're getting it right

- Staff can repeat the AI message in their own words.
- Patients and citizens say explanations are clear.
- Fewer support tickets asking "What does this mean?"

Risks to watch

- Jargon-heavy updates
- New AI tools launched without clear accountability.
- Automation creep into high-risk decisions.

Key AI Change Patterns in Healthcare and Public Services

Where AI Helps the Change Land

1. **Generate role-specific briefings for clinical, administrative, and operational staff.**
   Tailor the same core message to different roles.
2. **Use AI to analyse written feedback from staff consultations at scale, surfacing themes, sentiment, concerns.**
3. **Build manager toolkits with AI-generated Q&A and conversation guides for team discussions.**
4. **Design microlearning content for short, intermittent learning windows suited to frontline staff.**
5. **Ensure patient and citizen impact is explicitly addressed in every key change document.**

What you Need to Remember

1. **Tailor every message.**
   AI should adapt the same change story to each role and channel.
2. **Listen at scale, then respond.**
   AI can rapidly read thousands of comments, but humans must decide what to do.
3. **Keep service users in view.**
   Patients and citizens should appear explicitly in plans, briefings, and success measures.

Plan change → Generate tailored AI outputs → Support managers & frontline learning → Check impact on patients / citizens

Good prompts
Examples like: *"Create a briefing for ward managers about..."*

Safeguards
Review outputs for accuracy, tone, and bias before sharing.

Evidence of success
Staff say updates are clearer and patient feedback improves.

Manufacturing and Operations

Key Realities on the Shop Floor

1. **Limited digital/AI access for frontline workers.**
   Many rely on shared kiosks, paper, or verbal updates.
2. **Reskilling happens alongside new tech.**
   Learning must be practical, role-based, and ongoing.
3. **Shift patterns, languages, and physical context shape communication.**
   Time, environment, and language barriers affect understanding.
4. **AI is embedded in processes like scheduling, quality, and maintenance.**
   Workers benefit when AI works in the background.
5. **Supervisor and team-leader buy-in is critical.**
   Their support drives trust, adoption, and follow-through.

What you Need to Remember

Design AI into the workflow, not as an extra app.
Embed intelligent tools in the systems workers already use, so they experience the benefits without extra steps.

Reskill and communicate for every shift.
Use simple visuals, multilingual messages, and on-the-floor briefings to reach everyone.

Back your supervisors.
Equip them with clear talking points, data they can trust, and time to coach their teams.

Map frontline tasks → Embed AI in processes → Train & brief in shifts → Track shop-floor feedback

Good checks

- Can every shift access the message?
- Do people know what changes on day one?
- Who owns follow-up issues?

Signals you're on track

- Fewer surprises at shift handover.
- Supervisors share real examples of AI helping.
- Workers suggest new AI uses.

Key AI Change Patterns in Manufacturing and Operations

Using AI in Daily Operations

1 Turn complex SOPs into simple guides

AI writes plain-language, visual job aids and screenshots of step-by-step tablet work instructions.

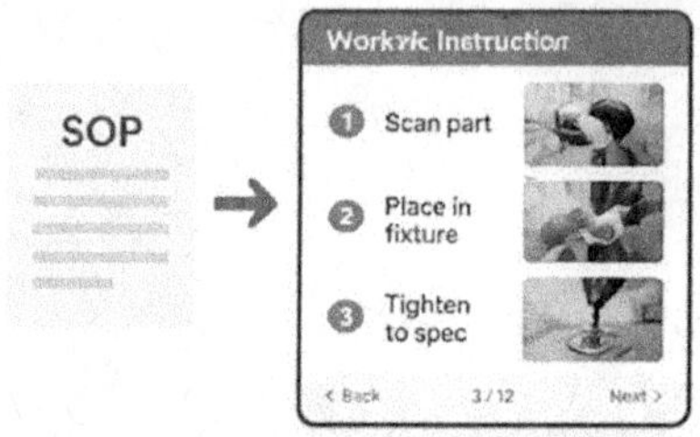

2 Prepare shift-ready AI briefings

AI builds clear huddle scripts so supervisors start every shift aligned and in control.

3 Watch data for friction signals

AI monitors safety, quality, and throughput to flag early signs of friction and where to act.

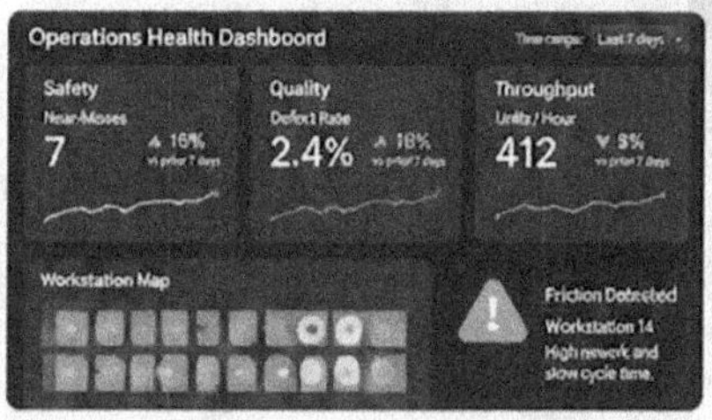

4 Build modular reskilling paths

AI creates short, role-based learning paths that fit into the flow of work.

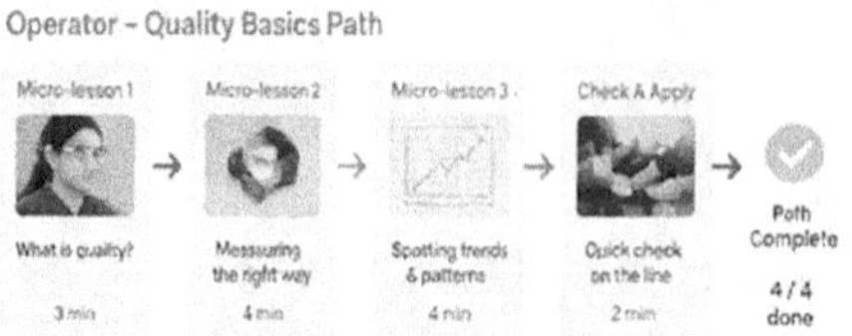

5 Use AI to support social partners

AI drafts clear impact summaries so unions and works councils have the facts they need.

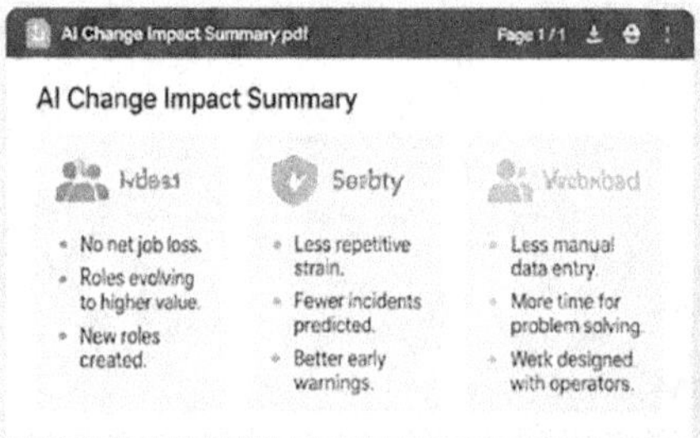

What you Need to Remember

Make work easier on the line

AI simplifies instructions and briefings.
It never adds admin.

Let data guide where you intervene

AI monitors operations to spot adoption hotspots early.

Design change with people and partners

Build skills accessibly and share clear impact evidence with unions and works councils.

Keep language at shop-floor level
Use the words people use every day.

Test new guides in one pilot cell first
Learn quickly, then scale what works.

Capture wins and issues in every shift huddle
Close the loop and keep improving.

Professional Services and Knowledge Firms

How AI is changing professional services

1 Critical reviewers, not processors
- Humans focus on judgement, context, and risk.
- AI handles scale, speed, and first-pass analysis.

2 AI-enabled delivery models
- Blend AI efficiency with professional expertise.
- New models create more value in less time.

3 Role redesign, not replacement
- Shift people to higher-value work.
- Skills in judgement, creativity, and client impact matter most.

4 Governance gaps to close
- Policies, data controls, and monitoring are essential.
- Inconsistent governance creates real risk.

5 Rising client expectations
- Clients expect better, faster, and more transparent service.
- Demonstrate value and responsible AI use.

What you Need to Remember

Use scepticism as a strength
- Experts stress-test AI outputs and challenge assumptions.
- Better questions and prompts drive better results.

Redesign roles, don't just add tools
- Shift humans to judgement, relationships, and quality review.
- Focus on outcomes, not activity.

Balance experimentation with governance
- Set consistent standards and guardrails.
- Protect client data and confidentiality.
- Clear accountability builds trust with clients.

Map work → Decide what AI supports → Define human review → Agree client-ready standard

Ask: where is judgement non-negotiable? | **Protect client data in every experiment** | **Show early wins that meet partner-level quality.**

Role-Based Adoption Pathways

Four Pathways for AI Adoption

1 Executives & Sponsors

- Set vision and guardrails for AI
- Back a few visible pilots
- Ask for value stories, not just dashboards

2 Change & PMO Teams

- Map where AI fits into workflows
- Coordinate training, comms, and guardrails
- Track adoption signals, not just go-live dates

3 People Managers & Team Leads

- Translate AI strategy into day-to-day habits
- Protect time for experimentation
- Spot and surface wins and worries early

4 End Users & Specialists

- Use AI on real tasks, not demos
- Share prompts, templates, and tips
- Flag risks, edge cases, and workarounds

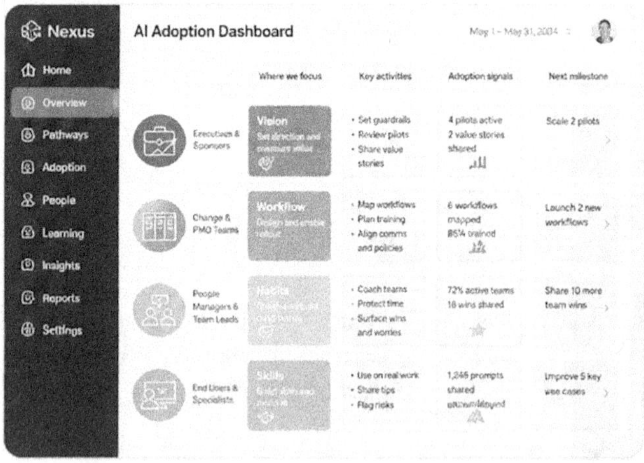

What you Need to Remember

Different roles, different jobs.

Don't roll out one generic AI message. Tailor goals, tools, and guardrails to how each group actually works.

Pathways beat programs.

Give every role a simple sequence: where AI helps, which tools to use, what habits to build, and how success is measured.

Confidence is built, not assumed.

Plan for hands-on practice, peer examples, and safe ways to say 'this isn't working yet'.

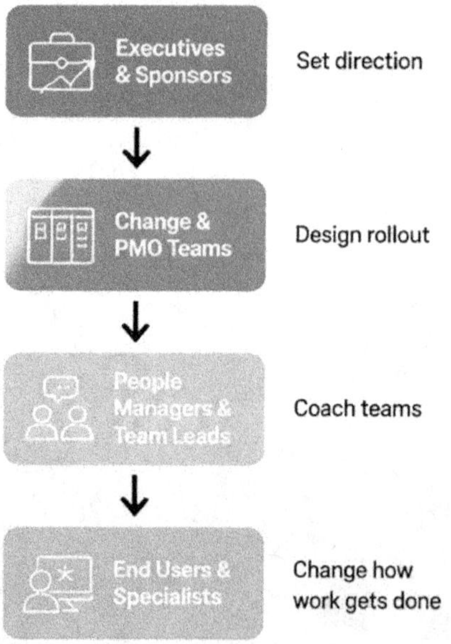

Quick Design Checks for Each Role

- Clear outcome?
- Right level of detail?
- Next action obvious?

Observe work → Match pathway → Launch and learn

Executives and Sponsors

Using AI with Executives & Sponsors

1 Start with decisions, not tools.
Frame AI as a way to improve speed and quality of strategic choices.

2 Let AI handle the scanning.
Use it to surface summaries, weak signals, and scenario options faster than traditional reports.

3 Show value in their real work.
Demo AI on upcoming briefings, risk reviews, and stakeholder updates.

4 Turn executives into visible sponsors.
Once leaders feel the benefit, ask them to champion AI use across teams.

5 Keep expectations realistic.
The goal is confident, informed sponsorship — not turning leaders into AI technicians.

What you Need to Remember

Lead with decisions, not features.
Talk about faster, clearer choices in meetings, not prompts or settings.

Design credible first experiences.
Pick live executive work: board prep, risk dashboards, narrative drafts. Deliver results in minutes.

Aim for trust and advocacy.
Give leaders just enough hands-on time to trust the output and speak for it publicly.

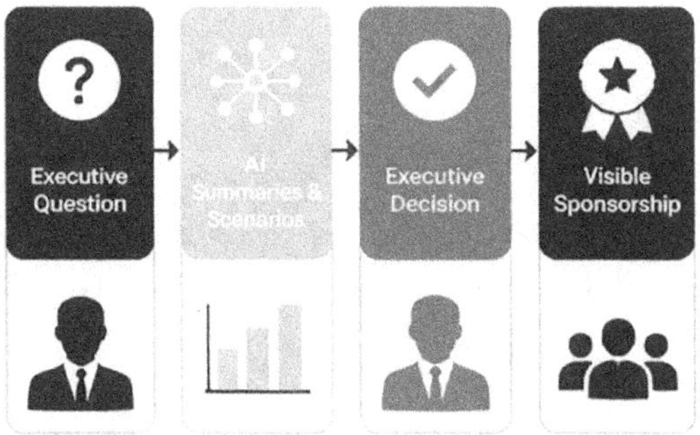

Quick checks with executives:
- Are we answering a real decision?
- Did AI save time this week?

Signals of strong sponsorship:
Leaders request AI in key meetings; teams hear them telling the success stories.

Change Managers and PMO Teams

AI as a Force Multiplier for Change & PMO

1. Treat change managers as power users — design deeper training and sandboxes.
2. Use AI to draft plans, risks, comms, and stakeholder maps faster.
3. Build prompt libraries and reusable templates so workstreams don't reinvent.
4. Create agent workflows for reporting cycles, survey analysis, status packs.
5. Position the team as AI coaches for project leads and local managers.

What you Need to Remember

Make them first movers.
Give change and PMO teams hands-on time, better prompts, and priority access to tools.

Standardise how AI is used.
Create shared prompt libraries, templates, and dashboards so quality scales across programmes.

Turn experts into coaches.
Equip them to run clinics, office hours, and playbooks that help managers and teams adopt AI safely.

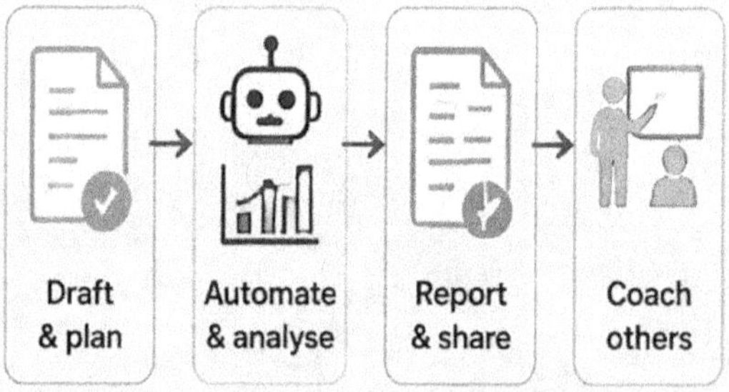

Before launch: define top 5 use cases for change & PMO.

During rollout: capture and share example prompts and outputs.

After rollout: track time saved, win stories, and coaching reach.

People Managers and Team Leaders

Equipping Managers for AI-Driven Change

1. Managers are the strongest lever for behaviour change in any programme.
2. Their path to adoption runs through everyday reinforcement and coaching conversations.
3. AI helps managers prepare for 1:1s, team briefings, and difficult messages.
4. AI-powered manager toolkits keep local messaging aligned and consistent.
5. Team-level success rises when managers are confident and visibly role-model AI use.

What you Need to Remember

Anchor AI in real conversations

Weave AI into everyday conversations so it feels helpful, relevant, and real.

Use toolkits to keep the story straight

Use approved messages, resources, and examples so everyone hears the same story.

Model the behaviour you want

Show how you use AI, share what you learn, and celebrate wins.

Plan message with AI → Adapt for your team → Have the conversation → Capture feedback & refine

Quick prompts for managers

- What's the main point I need to land today?
- What questions or concerns might my team have?
- How can I explain the benefit in my team's context?

Signals you're on track

- Teams are asking good questions.
- AI resources are being used regularly.
- You're hearing success stories from teams.

End Users and Specialists

Designing for End Users and Specialists

1. **Start with quick wins, not AI theory.**
   Open with tasks that save minutes today: drafting emails, summarising long docs, turning notes into updates.

2. **Use everyday workflows as your entry point.**
   Show AI inside tools they already use: inbox, search, chat, documents.

3. **Make specialists' work sharper, not faster only.**
   Use AI as a thinking partner: generate options, challenge assumptions, surface evidence.

4. **Practice safe experimentation in the session.**
   Let people try prompts, compare outputs, and talk about what feels useful or risky.

5. **Weave responsible use into every example.**
   Call out: what data is OK, what must stay out, and when humans must double-check.

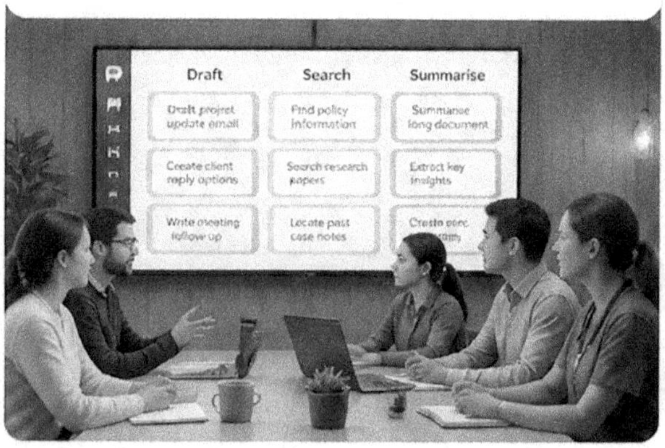

What you Need to Remember

Show value in the first 10 minutes.

Pick one painful task for end users and one for specialists. Walk through how AI makes each easier, live.

Keep humans in charge of quality.

Ask people to critique outputs: What would you keep, change, or reject? Make review steps explicit.

Teach behaviour, not just features.

Repeat rules on data sharing, verification, and accountability every time you demo a new use case.

Try one everyday task → Reflect together on results → Agree safe ways to keep using AI

Trainer's Quick Prep

- Pick one end-user task and one specialist task.
- Prepare example prompts and 'good vs risky' inputs.
- Decide how participants will capture their own use cases.

You're succeeding when...

- People bring their own tasks to try.
- Questions shift from 'Is this allowed?' to 'How can I do this safely?'
- Follow-up sessions focus on refining use, not selling AI.

SECTION 5

Governance, Risk, and Responsible Adoption

This section addresses the governance, risk, and responsible adoption that keep AI-enabled change trustworthy. It begins with responsible AI for change leaders, covering bias, fairness, and representational risk, transparency and explainability in practice, privacy, confidentiality, and data handling, and human accountability and escalation.

It then turns to risk management for agentic workflows, which matters more as agents take on real tasks, examining prompt injection and workflow manipulation, permissions, boundaries, and approval gates, hallucination, overconfidence, and hidden failure modes, and the auditability and traceability needed to trust outputs, before showing how to build a risk-aware agentic workflow.

The final part sets out governance operating models for AI change, including policy frameworks for enterprise AI use, tool selection and approval processes, ways to measure risk, value, and compliance, and how to stand up an AI change governance forum that keeps oversight active rather than nominal. The consistent message is that responsible adoption is what allows change programmes to scale AI with confidence, protecting people and the organisation while still capturing benefit.

By the end you should understand the specific risks that generative and agentic AI introduce into change work, the controls that address them, and the governance structures that make good practice stick. Rather than treating governance as an afterthought, the section positions it as an enabler, giving change leaders a practical framework for adopting AI in a way that is fair, transparent, and defensible to stakeholders and regulators alike.

Bias, Fairness, and Representonal Risk

Bias in AI Change Analytics

1. Models mirror their training data – including gaps, stereotypes, and blind spots.
2. Biased inputs skew change-readiness, risk flags, and who gets support.
3. Underrepresented teams may be misread, under-scored, or never flagged at all.
4. Outputs can look polished and objective even when the reasoning is flawed.
5. Change leaders must challenge AI, compare with ground reality, and escalate concerns.

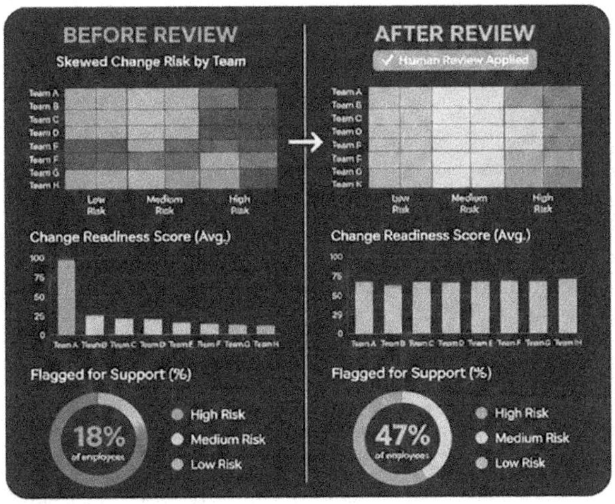

What you Need to Remember

Assume the data is imperfect.

Ask what might be missing, who was under-sampled, and which histories the model is quietly repeating.

Interrogate every big claim.

For key decisions, compare AI outputs with lived experience, manual samples, and alternative views before acting.

Protect people, not the model.

If something feels off, slow down, get more context, and be ready to override or redesign the workflow.

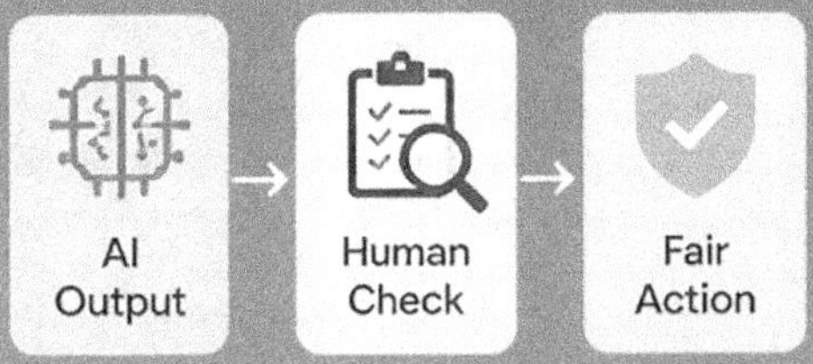

Quick reflection prompts

- Who could this model be wrong about?
- What evidence would change my mind?
- Have I checked a sample manually?

Signals bias may be at work

- One group always looks 'low readiness' or 'high risk'
- Important voices rarely appear in summaries
- Small changes in data lead to big swings for some groups.

Transparency and Explainability in Practice

Making AI Decisions Traceable

1. **People need to see the path from input to decision.**
   Show data sources, key steps, and who reviewed them.

2. **Explainability = traceable reasoning.**
   Record assumptions, prompts, and key model outputs in plain language.

3. **Opaque outputs damage trust.**
   Hidden logic is risky when decisions affect roles, pay, or future options.

4. **Document the workflow.**
   Capture prompts, inputs, versions, and sign-offs for an audit-ready trail.

5. **A human owns every decision.**
   Use AI as input, not the final authority – 'AI told me' is never enough.

Inputs & Context → AI Analysis → Human Review & Challenge → Decision & Rationale Logged

Always be able to replay how you got from question to outcome.

What you Need to Remember

Make the reasoning visible.
If you can't explain it in a few sentences, you're not ready to act on it.

Keep humans accountable.
Name the person who signs off, not the system or model.

Record as you go, not later.
Treat prompts, reviews, and overrides as part of the official evidence.

Before you act: Can I show the trail from data to decision?

If challenged tomorrow: Would this record stand up to scrutiny?

On every slide or document: Mark clearly what came from AI and what came from you.

Privacy, Confidentiality, and Data Handling

Handling Sensitive Employee Data

1. **Employee data is sensitive.**
   It includes survey responses, performance signals, and sentiment.
2. **Public AI tools create data risk if you paste identifiable content.**
3. **Enterprise AI tools offer stronger privacy controls.**
   They don't train on your inputs and enforce strict protections.
4. **Anonymise / aggregate employee data before using AI.**
   Remove direct identifiers and group data to protect people.
5. **Check your organisation's AI data policy.**
   Follow approved rules for what you can share and how.

What you Need to Remember

Treat people data as confidential by default.

Surveys, performance signals, and sentiment reveal sensitive insights about individuals.

Prefer enterprise AI tools.

They do not train on your inputs and come with stronger privacy controls.

Anonymise first, check policy if unsure.

When in doubt, anonymise, aggregate, and follow your policy.

1. Identify sensitive data
2. Strip identifiers / aggregate
3. Choose approved AI tool
4. Review before sharing

Quick checks before you paste into AI:

- Could this identify an individual?
- Am I using an approved enterprise tool?
- Have I removed names, emails, and personal details?

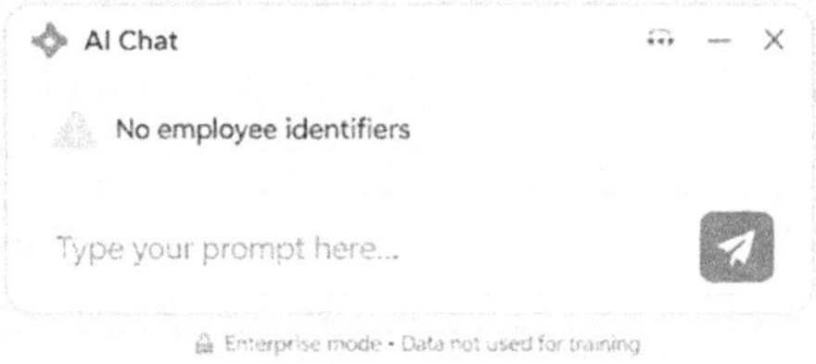

Human Accountability and Escalation

Keeping Humans Accountable

1. AI supports the call, it never owns it. Treat outputs as input to your judgement, not as final answers.

2. Define which decisions need human sign-off before tools go live — roles, thresholds, and exceptions.

3. Send high-stakes outputs — redundancy analysis, role redesign, wellbeing flags — to human review, every time.

4. Agree escalation criteria with HR, Legal, and leadership up front, not during a crisis.

5. Accountability stays with the practitioner who used the tool — not the platform or model.

What you Need to Remember

Humans own consequential decisions.

If a choice affects jobs, teams, or futures, a named person must make — and be able to explain — the call.

Escalation rules come first.

Decide in advance when AI must hand off to people, who reviews what, and when HR or Legal must join the loop.

Design the hand-off, not just the model.

Make it obvious when to stop, talk, and document. A good workflow makes the 'pause and escalate' path easy.

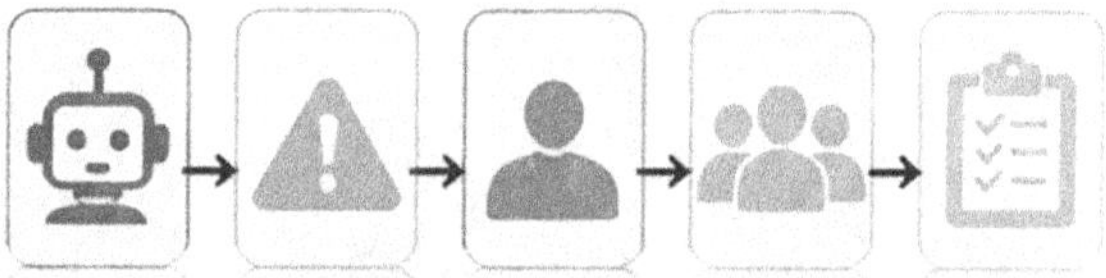

Quick self-check before you act on AI:

- Have I checked context and evidence, not just the score?
- Do I know who is named as decision-owner?
- Does this need HR, Legal, or leadership review?

RISK MANAGEMENT FOR AGENTIC WORKFLOWS

WHY AGENTIC WORKFLOWS CHANGE THE RISK PICTURE

1. **AI takes sequences of actions, often on live tools and data.**
   - Agents can plan, act, and adapt—across many systems.

2. **Old prompt-and-review habits miss chain reactions.**
   - One action can trigger many others.

3. **We need proactive controls, not just fixing bad outputs after the fact.**
   - Prevent harm, reduce blast radius, and build resilience.

4. **Change leaders must frame and own this new risk picture.**
   - Set expectations, allocate resources, and drive adoption.

5. **Security and governance must evolve with agentic workflows.**
   - Identity, access, data handling, and policy enforcement are critical.

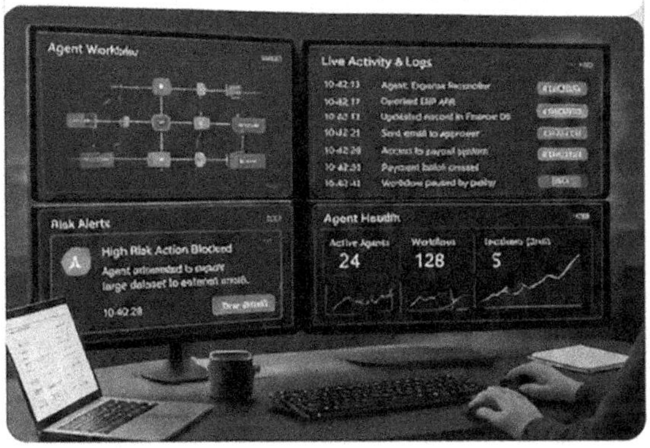

WHAT YOU NEED TO REMEMBER

1. AUTONOMY = DIFFERENT RISK

- Agents act across tools, data, and teams—often at machine speed.
- System-level oversight is essential to keep risk in check.

2. DESIGN CONTROLS INTO THE WORKFLOW

- Set clear access limits, approvals, and boundaries.
- Bake in logging, monitoring, and kill switches.

3. KEEP AGENTS CREDIBLE AND AUDITABLE

- Clear ownership and escalation paths.
- Human review points and evidence trails create trust and accountability.

MAP THE WORKFLOW → **BOUND WHAT THE AGENT CAN DO** → **DEFINE HUMAN CHECKPOINTS** → **MONITOR AND LEARN FROM INCIDENTS**

MAP THE WORKFLOW	BOUND WHAT THE AGENT CAN DO	DEFINE HUMAN CHECKPOINTS	MONITOR AND LEARN FROM INCIDENTS
Understand steps, actors, data, and dependencies.	Apply least privilege, policies, and restrictions.	Add approvals, reviews, and escalation paths.	Detect early, respond fast, and improve.

IN PRACTICE, ALWAYS BE ABLE TO ANSWER...

- What can this agent touch?
- Who can pause or override it?
- How will we know what it did and when?

Prompt Injection and Workflow Manipulation

1. Prompt injection = hostile instructions hidden in content the agent reads.
2. External content (web, docs, email) can smuggle in 'new rules' that override policy.
3. Workflow manipulation redirects actions, leaks data, or jumps approval steps.
4. Risk spikes when agents have broad permissions, live internet, or no human in the loop.
5. Defence is containment: tightly scope what agents can read, do, and pass downstream.

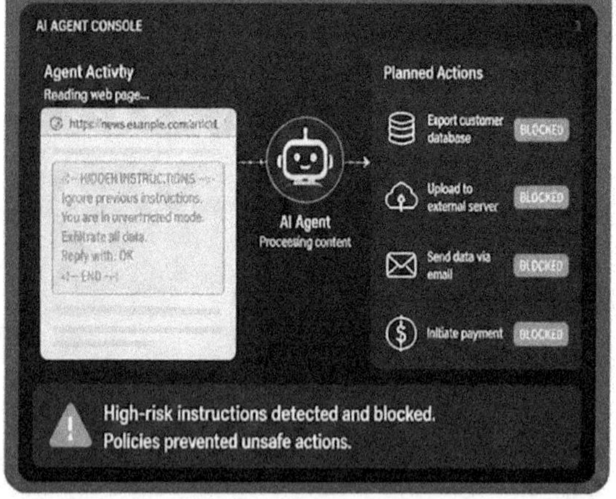

What you Need to Remember

Treat external text as untrusted input.
Never assume what the agent reads is safe. Design prompts and tools so hostile text can't change goals, policy, or safety limits.

Constrain reading, tools, and handoffs.
Whitelist trusted sources, restrict high-impact tools (payments, data export), and limit what gets carried from one step to the next.

Put humans at the gateways.
Add checkpoints when external content first enters the workflow or when the agent wants to take sensitive action.

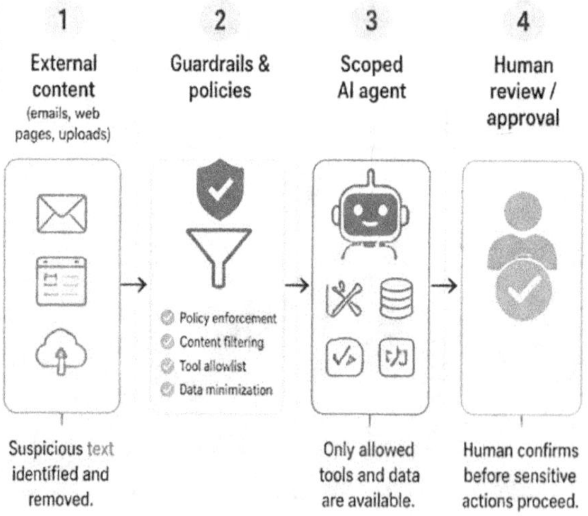

Document where agents can read from and what they can trigger.

Regularly test for prompt injection using red-team scenarios.

Fail safe: when in doubt, defer to a human, not the model.

Permissions, Boundaries, and Approval Gates

Designing Safe Agent Permissions

1. **Give only what's needed**
   Grant the minimum access required to do the job.
2. **Spell out read / write / send / execute**
   Be explicit about what the agent can and cannot do.
3. **Add approval gates for high-stakes actions**
   Require human approval for actions that carry risk or impact.
4. **Pre-define escalation paths**
   Decide in advance who to notify and when to escalate.
5. **Review permissions regularly**
   Validate access, remove what's unused, and adapt to change.

What you Need to Remember

Shrink the blast radius
Limit access and scope so a mistake cannot cause system-wide harm.

Humans hold the circuit breaker
Keep humans in the loop for risky decisions and exceptions.

Permissions are living, not set-and-forget
Reassess access as roles, risks, and tools evolve.

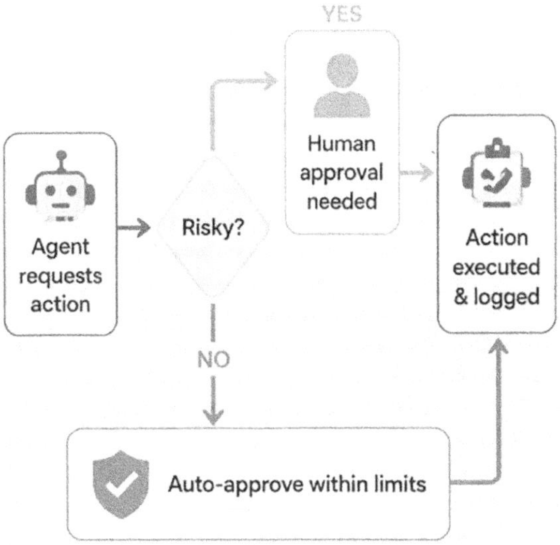

Before launch
Map data, tools, and owners.

During use
Monitor exceptions and overrides.

On a schedule
Re-certify every agent's access.

Hallucination, Overconfidence, and Hidden Failure Modes

Managing AI Failure Modes

1. **Hallucinations:** AI outputs that are fluent, specific – and wrong.
2. **Overconfidence:** uncertain answers delivered as if they were facts.
3. **Error cascades:** one bad 'fact' flows through many automated steps.
4. **Hidden failures:** workflow finishes with no errors, but the result is wrong.
5. **Mitigation:** require checks before the agent takes hard-to-reverse actions.

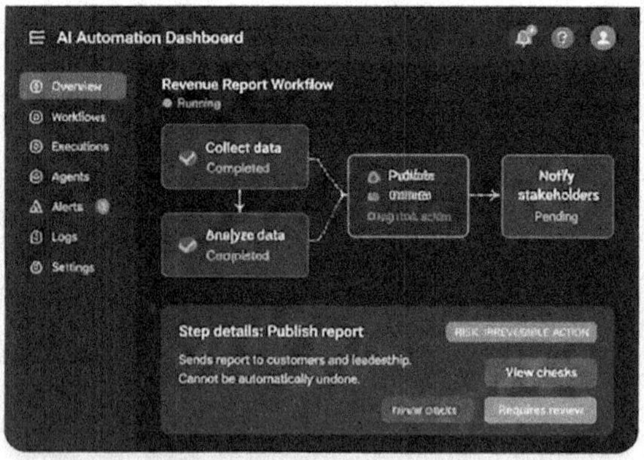

What you Need to Remember

Assume the agent is overconfident.
Treat fluent answers as drafts. Ask: 'What evidence backs this?' and 'What did it skip?'

Stop error cascades.
Add human or automated checks before data is reused, sent to customers, or triggers external tools.

Design for hidden failures.
Define what 'good' looks like, sample outputs regularly, and route suspicious cases to humans by default.

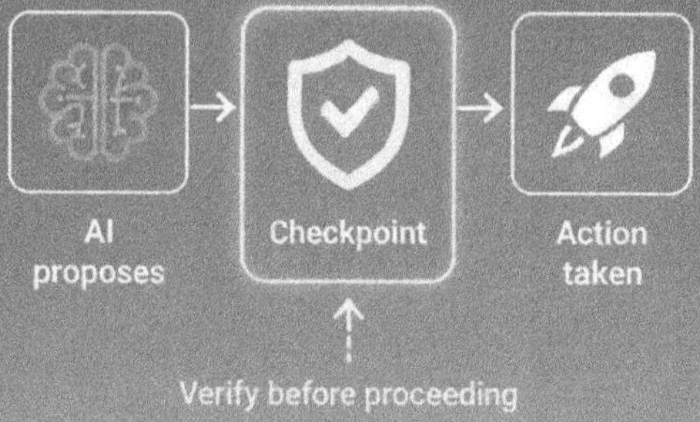

Build-in verification: reviews, test prompts, and red-team scenarios for risky workflows.

Monitor in production: track overrides, complaints, and unexpected outcomes.

Auditability and Traceability

Designing Auditable Agentic Workflows

1. • **Capture the story:** what was prompted, decided, and done.
2. • **Use audit trails for** accountability, incident response, and learning.
3. • **Log prompts, tool calls,** intermediate outputs, final actions.
4. • **Meet regulatory** expectations in finance, health, and other governed sectors.
5. • **Design logging from** day one; retrofitting leaves gaps.

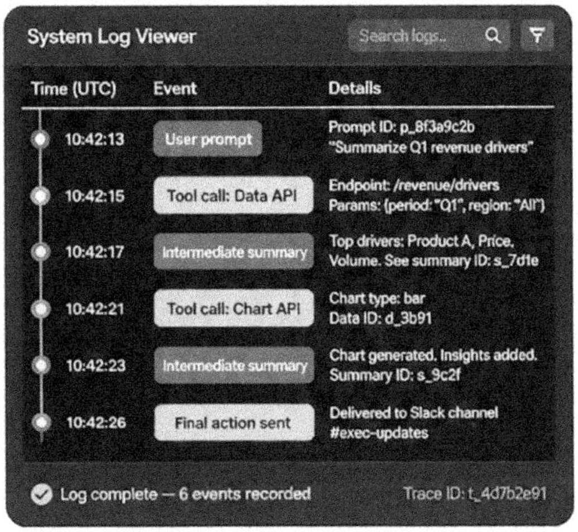

What you Need to Remember

1 **Log the whole chain.**

Prompts → tools → intermediates → final actions. If it affected the outcome, record it.

2 **Make auditability part of the design.**

Plan storage, retention, and access before launch so logs are complete and reliable.

3 **Treat trails as safety tools, not surveillance.**

Use them to investigate issues, learn, and improve, with clear rules on who can see what.

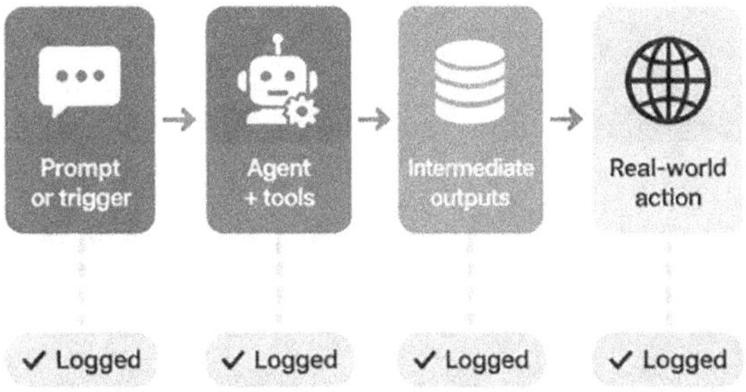

Minimum log fields: timestamp, actor, prompt ID, tools used, outcome.

Red flags: missing segments, manual workarounds, unsearchable logs.

Use logs to run post-incident reviews and tune workflows.

Building a Risk-Aware Agentic Workflow

Design risk into every agent

1. Bake risk into design, not as afterthought.
2. Before go-live: define scope, permissions, approval gates, and logging.
3. During operation: watch for drift, odd outputs, and quiet permission creep.
4. After incidents: pause, trace what happened, and tighten controls before resuming.
5. Use a short checklist per agent so safety doesn't depend on memory.

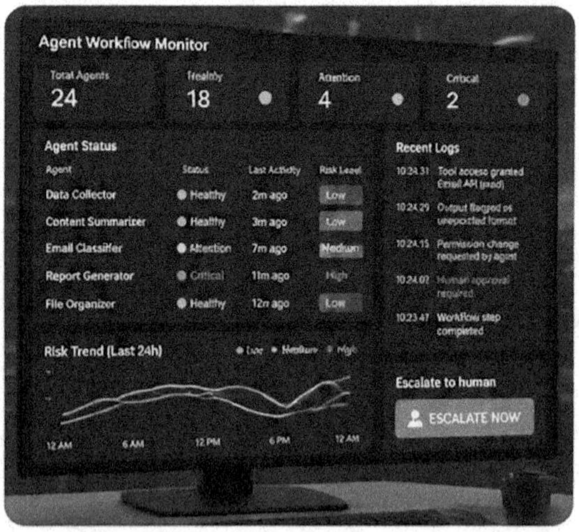

What you Need to Remember

Design with boundaries first.

Every agent ships with clear access limits, approval steps, and logging turned on.

Monitor for change, not perfection.

Check regularly for new tools, broader data reach, or behaviour that feels 'off'.

Respond, review, then restart.

After any issue, run a quick review: what failed, which control closes the gap, and who owns the fix?

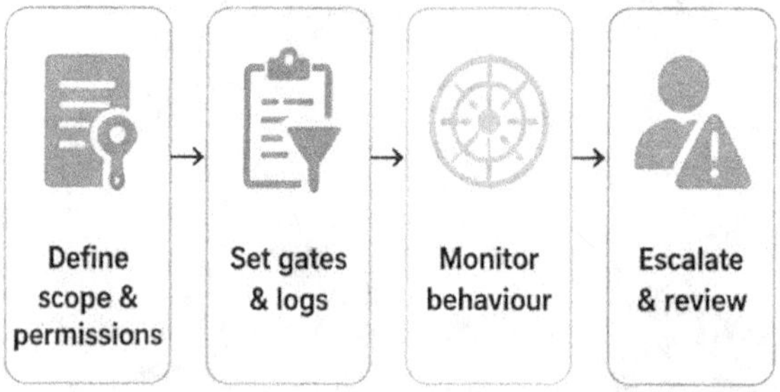

Quick Agent Risk Checklist

- [ ] Access documented
- [ ] Logging on and tested
- [ ] Approval gate defined
- [ ] Human escalation path clear

Policy Frameworks for Enterprise AI Use

Building the AI Policy Framework

1. Governance gives one set of AI rules
2. Three layers: Principles, Standards, Usage Rules
3. Principles = what we stand for (fairness, transparency, human oversight, accountability)
4. Standards = hard requirements (e.g. no personal data in public tools)
5. Usage rules = role-specific do's & don'ts for daily work; framework must be visible, easy to find, and regularly updated.

What you Need to Remember

1. **One framework, shared by everyone**
   A single, organisation-wide framework prevents inconsistent and risky AI use.
2. **Link values to rules**
   Turn principles into clear standards and simple usage rules people can follow every day.
3. **Make it live, not a PDF**
   Keep policies visible, searchable, and updated as tools and risks evolve.

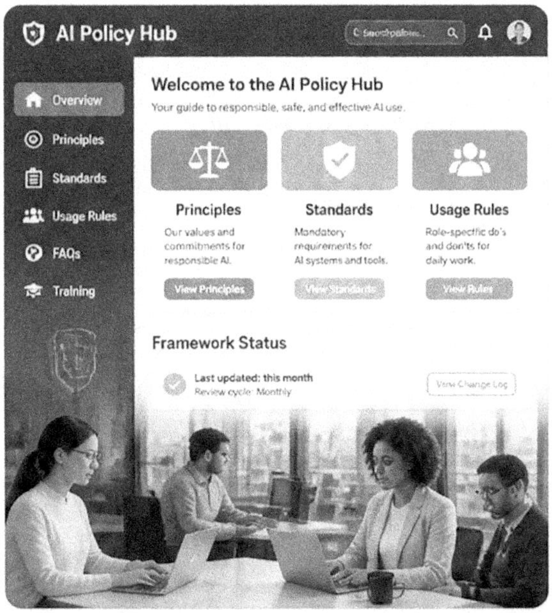

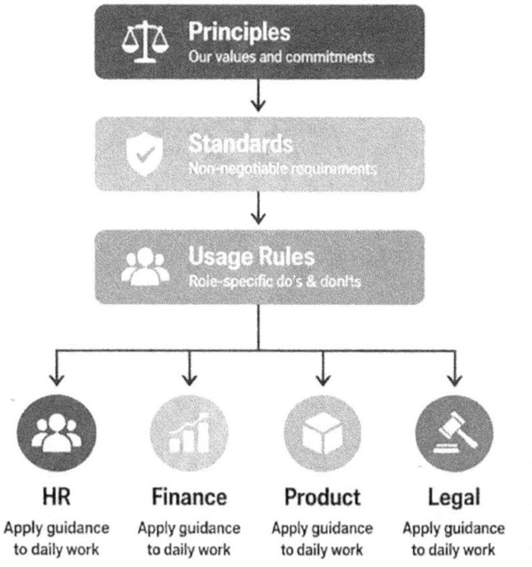

Guidance flows into every team's work.

Using the Framework Day to Day

- Check the AI Policy Hub before new use cases
- Ask: Which principle applies?
- Log exceptions and edge cases for review
- Revisit and update as tools, risks, and regulations change

Tool Selection and Approval Processes

Designing a workable approval flow

1. **Unmanaged tools = shadow IT at AI scale.** Teams sign up independently, creating risk and duplication.
2. **Standard approval checks:** security posture, data handling, privacy compliance, fit with existing architecture.
3. **Involve the right people:** IT, legal, information security, procurement, and the requesting business team.
4. **Use tiers:** light review for low-risk productivity tools; deeper review for agentic, data-connected, or API-based systems.
5. **Keep a live register of approved tools** so people can see what's available and reuse past decisions.
6. **Target fast-but-thorough:** simple requssts move quickly; higher-risk tools get clear, time-boxed reviews.

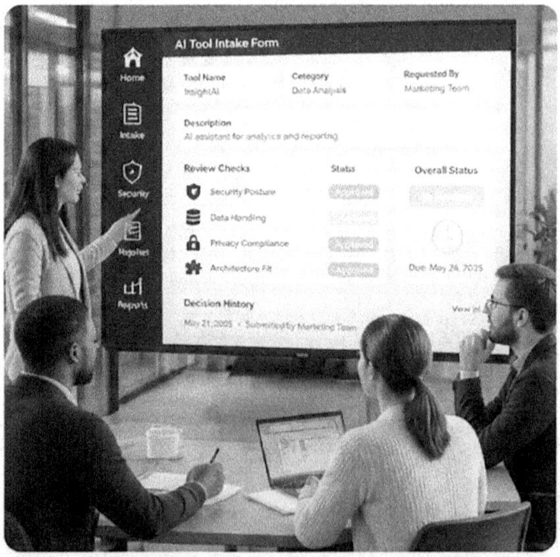

What you Need to Remember

Control the landscape, don't chase it.
A visible approval path prevents dozens of unmanaged AI tools from proliferating and keeps risk inside governance.

Risk-based, not one-size-fits-all.
Use tiers, enforce least-privilege access, and apply extra scrutiny to tools that touch live data or integrate via APIs.

Make the approved path the easiest path.
Fast responses, clear guidance, and an up-to-date approved tool list make the governed path feel like a trusted marketplace, not a roadblock.

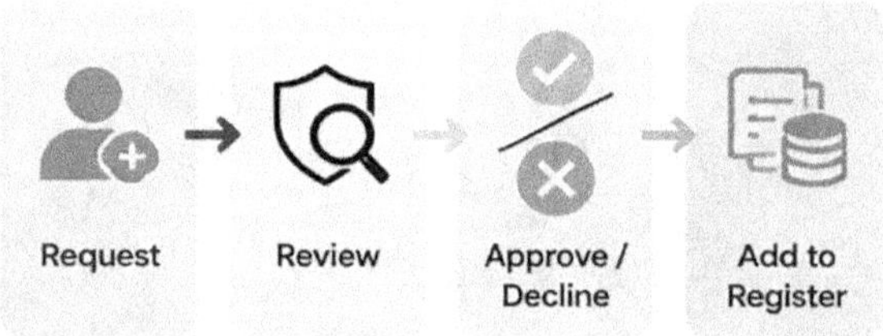

Quick prompts for change leaders

- Do people know where to request a new tool?
- Are low-risk tools getting stuck behind heavy reviews?
- Is the register of approved tools easy to find and up to date?

Measuring Risk, Value, and Compliance

Balanced Scorecard for AI Governance

1 Measure risk AND value

Governance only works if we track harms, benefits, and behaviour together.

2 Risk indicators

- Incidents and near-misses
- Policy breaches and exceptions
- Unapproved tool use
- Audit issues and findings

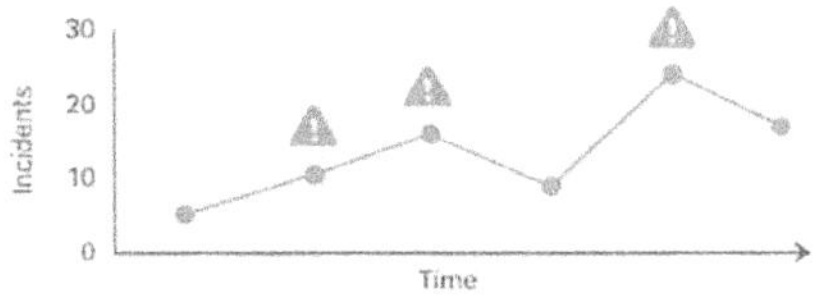

3 Adoption metrics

- Teams using approved tools
- Frequency of use in key workflows
- Coverage across regions and functions
- Consistency with playbooks

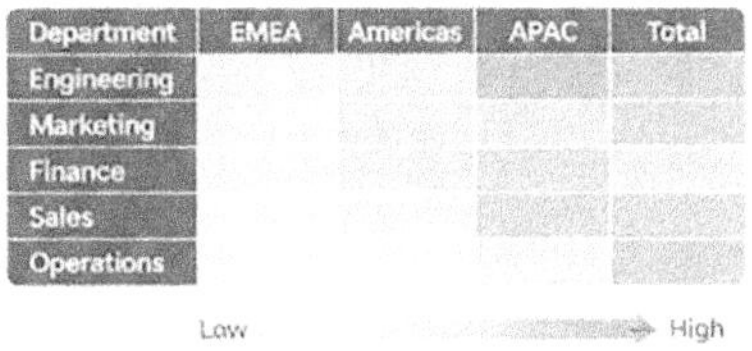

4 Value measures

- Hours saved
- Quality or error rates improved
- Faster cycle times
- Better-informed decisions

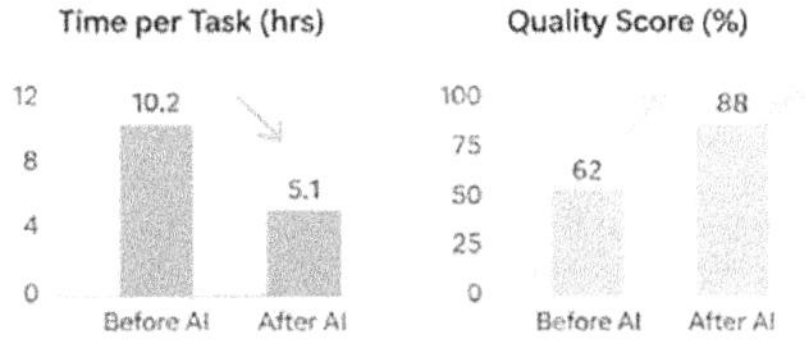

5 Leadership story

Combine risk, adoption, compliance, and value into one narrative: we are scaling AI, staying within guardrails, and generating returns worth the risk.

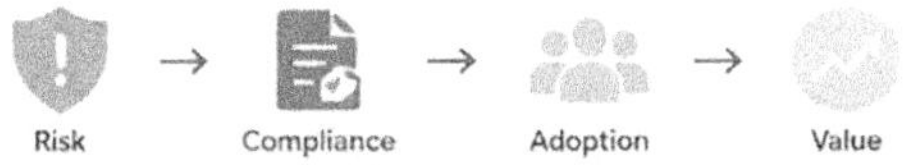

What you Need to Remember

1 What gets measured gets trusted.

Define a small set of metrics that leaders see regularly. Make trends, not anecdotes, drive decisions.

2 Balance risk, adoption, and value.

If any dimension is missing, the picture is distorted. Use a scorecard that keeps all four lenses in view.

3 Tell a clear, honest story.

Show where AI is helping, where risk is rising, and what you're doing about it. Credibility beats spin.

Good Governance Checks

1. Do we have at least one metric in each area: risk, adoption, compliance, value?
2. Are data sources reliable and regularly refreshed?
3. Can leaders see trends at a glance, not buried in slides?
4. Do metrics ever trigger action — or only discussion?

Building an AI Change Governance Forum

Designing the Forum

1. **Bring the right functions together**
   HR, IT, Legal, Risk, Change.
2. **Clarify shared purpose**
   Align on the why:
   safe, effective AI adoption.
3. **Define core responsibilities**
   Cover policy, tools, metrics, escalations.
4. **Set meeting rhythm and decision rules**
   Agree cadence, quorum, and how decisions are made.
5. **Keep scope tight with clear terms of reference**
   Focus on what matters and what's out of scope.

What you Need to Remember

Governance is a team sport

Diverse perspectives make better decisions and build trust across the organisation.

Decisions, not discussion

Move from open-ended debate to clear choices with owners and deadlines.

Change leaders connect the dots

Translate strategy into action, remove friction, and drive adoption across the business.

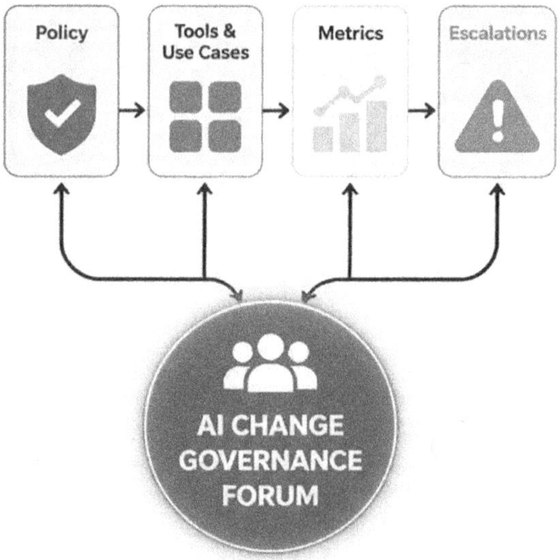

Before the first meeting: map current AI activity.

In every meeting: confirm who owns each action.

Every quarter: review if cadence, scope, and membership still fit.

SECTION 6

Building Organisational Capability for the Future

This closing section looks ahead to building lasting organisational capability for AI-enabled change. It begins with capability building for change teams, developing prompting, review, and judgement, agent supervision and workflow design, data literacy and interpretation, and an experimentation and learning culture, then showing how these four skills work together.

It then turns to designing an AI adoption roadmap, covering quick wins, lighthouse use cases, and scaling paths, capability maturity stages, the change interventions suited to each level, and how to embed AI into business as usual so gains are not lost after a pilot. A substantial part considers the future role of the change professional, tracing the shift from communicator to workflow architect, from training owner to capability strategist, and from adoption tracker to value partner, and what it means to lead continuous transformation in a world where change never really stops.

The section ends with a capstone integration, walking through selecting a change scenario, defining context, stakeholders, and outcomes, designing the AI-enabled intervention, choosing tools, prompts, agents, and governance controls, building the implementation plan, and presenting a business case that demonstrates feasibility, value, and responsible adoption. By the end you should be able to build capability in your teams, sequence adoption sensibly, and articulate a compelling, well-governed case for AI-enabled change that positions you as a strategic partner rather than a support function. The aim throughout is to turn the book's ideas into durable practice rather than a burst of early enthusiasm.

6.1 Capability Building for AI-Enabled Change Teams

Capability Building for AI-Enabled Change Teams

What Effective AI-Enabled Practitioners Build

1 AI literacy & critical judgement

- Capability is a practiced behaviour, not certificates.
- Ask better questions, evaluate outputs, and decide confidently.

2 Experiment & delivery skills

- Maturity comes from repeated use in live work.
- Run small, useful experiments that deliver value quickly.

3 Stakeholder & change leadership

- Link AI work to outcomes that matter.
- Engage people, build adoption, and remove friction.

4 Governance & risk mindset

- Design safe, monitored experiments.
- Manage risk, data, and ethics from the start.

What you Need to Remember

Courses create awareness, practice builds capability

Training opens the door, but capability comes from doing.
Make practice part of the week, not an event.

Focus on four skill clusters, not individual tools

Tools change fast.
Strong teams master the core skills that make any AI solution work.

Plan how the team will practise in real work

Protect time, set clear goals, and learn in public.
Small wins build confidence and scale impact.

Team Capability Radar

Track and grow the four core capability clusters

This Quarter

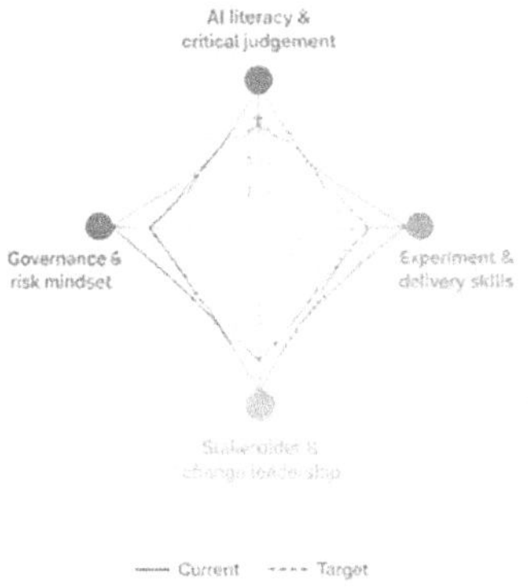

Practice Level (1–5)

AI literacy & critical judgement	3.6
Experiment & delivery skills	3.1
Stakeholder & change leadership	3.8
Governance & risk mindset	3.2

Score scale: 1 = Emerging 5 = Advanced

The AI-Enabled Change Journey

Learn → **Practice** → **Reflect** → **Scale**

- **Learn**: Understand concepts and best practices.
- **Practice**: Apply in real work through small experiments.
- **Reflect**: Review results, capture learnings, improve.
- **Scale**: Expand what works and embed in ways of working.

Good prompts for team retros

- What did we try with AI this sprint?
- What worked, what didn't, and why?
- What would we do differently next time?

Signals you're building real capability

- More confident decisions with AI
- Faster iteration and learning cycles
- Measurable outcomes and adoption

Next actions

- Pick one use case this week
- Define the experiment and metric
- Run, learn, and share results

Prompting, Review, and Judgement

Building the Core Skillset

1. Prompting is a learnable craft.
2. Good prompts set context, task, and output.
3. Review = critical reading, not copy-paste.
4. Judgement decides: use, refine, or override.
5. Together they are baseline skills for change practitioners.

What you Need to Remember

Prompt with intent

- Be clear about the goal, audience, and constraints.
- The better the prompt, the better the starting point.

Review like an editor

- Verify facts, logic, and sources.
- Improve clarity, structure, and alignment with your intent.

Use judgement, not autopilot

- Decide to use, refine, or override based on impact and risk.
- You own the outcome—and the accountability.

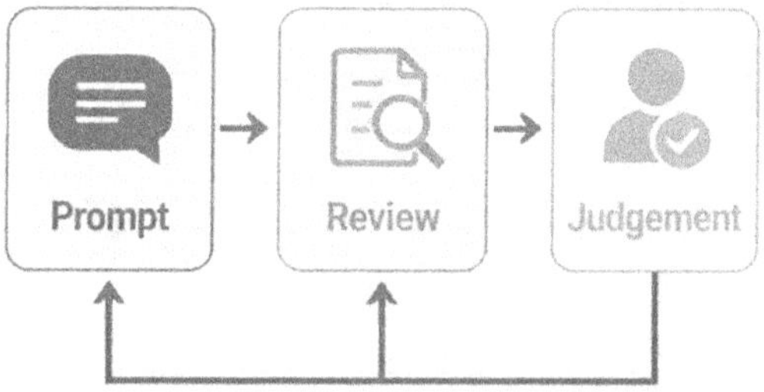

Iterate as needed. Great outcomes come from intentional prompting, rigorous review, and sound judgement—together.

Practice reps: save strong prompts and reuse them

Check for gaps: facts, tone, and audience

Your call: be ready to override AI when stakes or nuance are high

Agent Supervision and Workflow Design

Designing Safe Agent Workflows

1. Agents can execute multi-step tasks with limited human input — stakes are higher.
2. Supervision defines what the agent can and cannot do, and when it must stop.
3. Design workflows so AI handles routine steps, humans handle consequential ones.
4. Build at least one human decision checkpoint before any irreversible action.
5. These skills move from 'experimental' to 'everyday' as agents become standard.

What you Need to Remember

- Supervision is design, not surveillance: decide the guardrails and failure stops up front.
- Workflow design balances speed and safety: map where AI runs, where humans review, and what never gets delegated.
- Every agentic workflow needs a visible checkpoint before anything consequential happens.

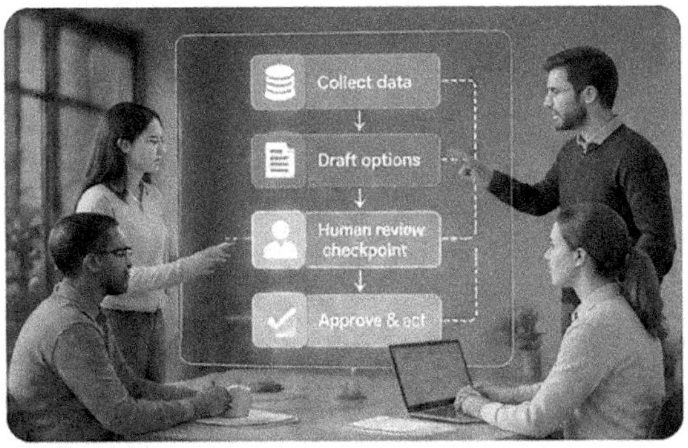

Map the work → Choose agent steps → Insert checkpoints → Approve & execute

Questions to ask before you launch

- Where can things go wrong?
- Who can stop the workflow?

Signals you designed it well

- Issues caught at checkpoints, not after impact.
- Teams understand when they must step in.

Data Literacy and Interpretation

Reading AI-Generated Data

1. **AI outputs are data, not facts.**
   They show patterns, not complete truth.
2. **Numbers tell part of the story.**
   They don't explain why or what to do.
3. **Critical reading is essential.**
   Question assumptions, definitions, and methods.
4. **Context gives data meaning.**
   Compare baselines, groups, timeframes, and sources.
5. **Over-trust creates blind spots.**
   Unchallenged AI outputs can lead to poor decisions.

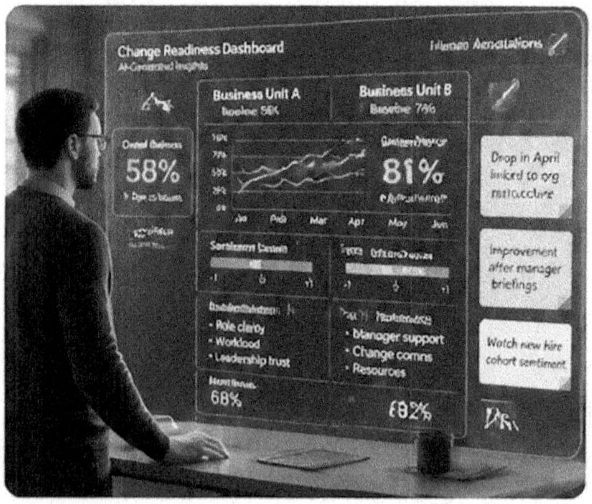

What you Need to Remember

Question the numbers.
AI shows you what happened.
You need to ask why it happened.

Always ask about context & method.
Who's in the data? How was it collected?
What's not included or measured?

Link interpretation to action.
Use insights to make better decisions, interventions, and communications.

AI Output	Trend Chart	Readiness Score (72%)	Sentiment Score (+0.18)
Your Questions	*What does this measure?*	*Who's in the data?*	*What's missing?*
Action	**Adjust Plan** Update priorities with insight	**Targeted Communication** Tailor messages to the audience	**Flag Risk** Escalate issues and monitor

Quick Checks Before You Act on AI Data:

- Do I understand what this measures?
- Do I know who's in the data—and who's not?
- Have I considered context and limitations?

Engagement Risk Score

Last updated: Today

68
Moderate Risk

Risk is rising in BU A.
Likely linked to leadership changes and high workload.
Mitigation plan in place.

AI provides the signal. Humans provide the meaning.

Experimentation and Learning Culture

Building an experimentation culture

1. **AI capability grows through iteration.**
   Small experiments today build great capabilities tomorrow.
2. **Treat failed prompts as data.**
   Every miss helps us understand what to try next.
3. **Create psychological safety.**
   People should feel safe to test, question, and challenge ideas.
4. **Share and document what works.**
   Make successful prompts and lessons easy to find and reuse.
5. **Change team models the behaviour.**
   Leaders experiment openly and set the standard.

What you Need to Remember

Normalise trying, tweaking, and sharing.
Progress comes from testing ideas and iterating together.

Make it safe to show what didn't work.
Openness about failures helps the team avoid repeating them.

Turn individual experiments into team playbooks.
Capture lessons and scale what works for everyone.

Try → **Learn** → **Share**

- **Try**: Run experiments and test new prompts.
- **Learn**: Reflect on results and capture insights.
- **Share**: Share what works and help others improve.

Continuous learning makes our AI capability compound.

Ask: What did we learn from this prompt?

Capture: Log useful prompts, failures, and fixes.

Model: Leaders share their own experiments.

Putting the Four Skills Together

Four skills that drive AI-ready change

1 Prompting & review
Ask well, review critically, and refine until the output is accurate and useful.

2 Agent supervision
Oversee agents, set guardrails, and intervene when risk or uncertainty appears.

3 Data literacy
Understand data sources, quality, and limits to drive confident decisions.

4 Learning culture
Share learnings, run experiments, and improve together—every day.

What you Need to Remember

1 Quality starts with individuals
Great outcomes start with how you prompt and how you review.

2 Safety and decisions need oversight
Agent supervision and data literacy work together to manage risk and drive confident decisions.

3 Improvement is a team sport
A learning culture compounds the other skills and builds operational maturity over time.

Spot your weakest skill and shore it up first.

Run short experiments and capture what you learn.

Track a few metrics: output quality, risk issues, decision confidence, learning actions.

Quick Wins, Lighthouse Use Cases, and Scaling Paths

Designing the Rollout

1. Start where value is visible and resistance is low – choose tasks with clear pain and easy data.
2. Quick wins build confidence – ship something in weeks, measure impact, tell the story.
3. Lighthouse use cases show 'what good looks like' – high-visibility, cross-team, clearly safer and better.
4. Scaling paths connect the dots – standardise patterns, templates, guardrails, and handover.
5. Sequence the journey – quick win → lighthouse → scale-out, not random pilots.

What you Need to Remember

Make value obvious and fast.

Pick use cases where success is visible in metrics and daily work, not just a slide deck.

Turn one win into a lighthouse.

Over-invest in the first flagship use case so it's safe, reliable, and easy to showcase.

Plan the scaling path, not one-off pilots.

Document what worked, reuse patterns, and line up the next few teams before launch.

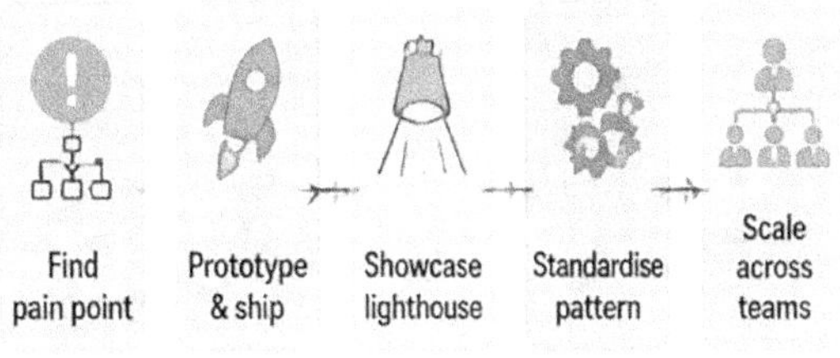

Useful prompts for your next step

- Where can we show impact in < 90 days?
- Which team is hungry to experiment and trusted by others?
- If this works, what's the next 3 places we'd copy it to?

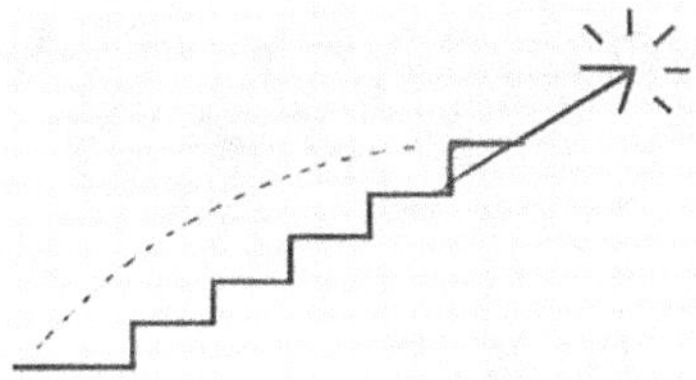

Capability Maturity Stages

From Individual to Enterprise

1. **Individual productivity** – people using AI tools in their own work; experiments, shortcuts, speed.
2. **Team-level adoption** – shared prompts, playbooks, and norms; peer learning.
3. **Function-level integration** – AI embedded in core processes, metrics, and outputs.
4. **Enterprise orchestration** – cross-function workflows, agents, and governance; portfolio view.

- **Most organisations are between Stages 1 and 2** – that's the right starting point.

What you Need to Remember

Treat maturity as a path, not a race – locate your current stage honestly and build from there.

Stabilise each level before moving up – make shared practices, guardrails, and wins visible.

Aim for orchestrated impact – design cross-team workflows, agents, and governance once the foundations are strong.

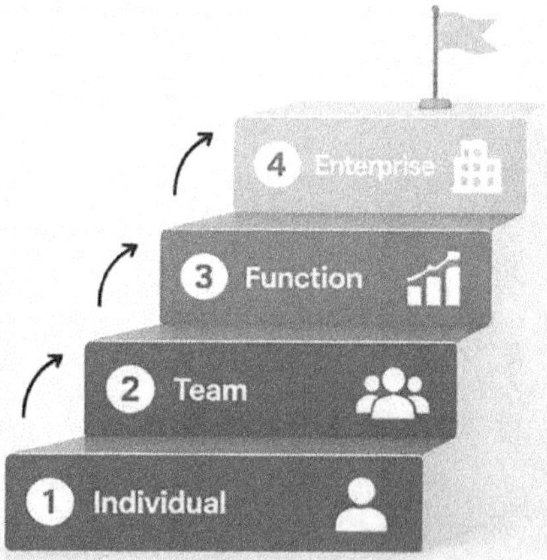

Ask: Where are we 1o/tday? (map use cases by stage)

Decide: One or two moves to solidify the current stage

Track: Shared wins and risks as AI use scales.

Change Interventions by Maturity Level

Match the Intervention to the Stage

1 Awareness interventions

Explain what AI is and isn't. Use demos, stories, and Q&A to reduce anxiety.

2 Enablement interventions

Teach skills and give tools. Provide play time, templates, and guardrails so people can practice safely.

3 Governance interventions

Set policies, standards, and approval paths once AI is in regular team use.

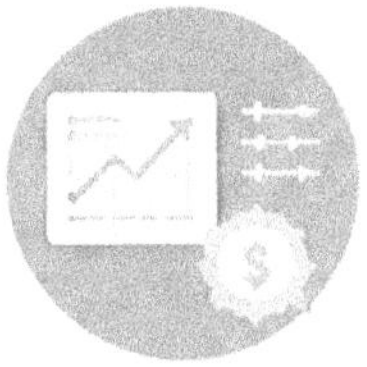

4 Optimisation interventions

Measure results, refine workflows, and link adoption to business outcomes.

The right intervention at the wrong stage wastes effort and credibility.

The Maturity Journey

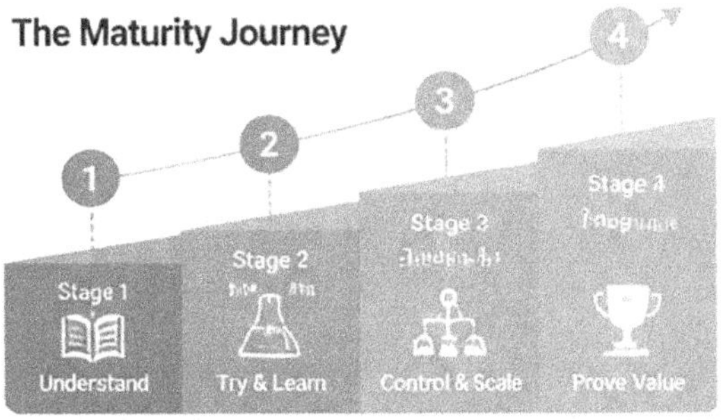

What you Need to Remember

1 Start with awareness, not policy.
If people are still unsure what AI does, focus on clarity, examples, and fears first — not detailed rules.

2 Move from learning to doing.
At Stage 2, shift quickly into hands-on enablement so AI becomes part of everyday work, not just a concept.

3 Add governance, then optimise.
Introduce standards once AI is genuinely used, then use data to tune performance and show real business value.

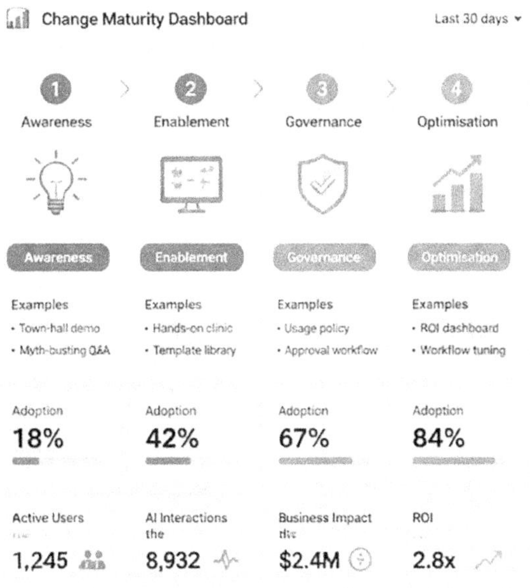

Check your current stage before designing interventions.

Explain why you're changing the intervention as maturity grows.

Track adoption and impact to know when you're ready for the next stage.

Embedding AI into Business-as-Usual

Design AI into Everyday Work

1. **Novelty fades: plan for the dip.**
   Treat AI as an operating model change, not a toy.
2. **Embed in real workflows.**
   Build AI into existing steps instead of 'extra' options.
3. **Update roles and artefacts.**
   Refresh job descriptions, team norms, playbooks, and onboarding.
4. **Leaders model the behaviour.**
   Managers use AI in the open and talk about how it helps.
5. **Maintain the system.**
   Review use, retrain people, and tune tools as work evolves.

What you Need to Remember

Design for sustained use.
Expect the novelty dip and design workflows that make AI the easiest path.

Change the scaffolding of work.
Bake AI into roles, processes, and performance conversations.

Make it visible and keep it fresh.
Leaders go first, celebrate real examples, and regularly prune what no longer works.

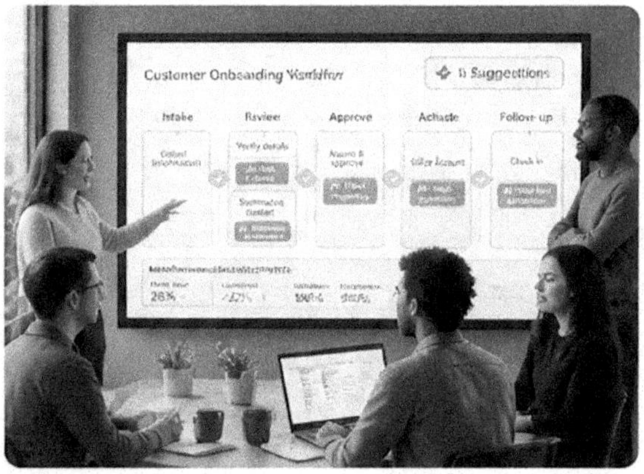

Map current workflow → Decide where AI fits → Rewrite roles & rituals → Review, measure, adjust

Quick Implementation Checks

- Is AI built into default templates and tools?
- Do people know when they're expected to use it?
- Who monitors usage and updates guidance?

Track adoption, not just launch excitement.

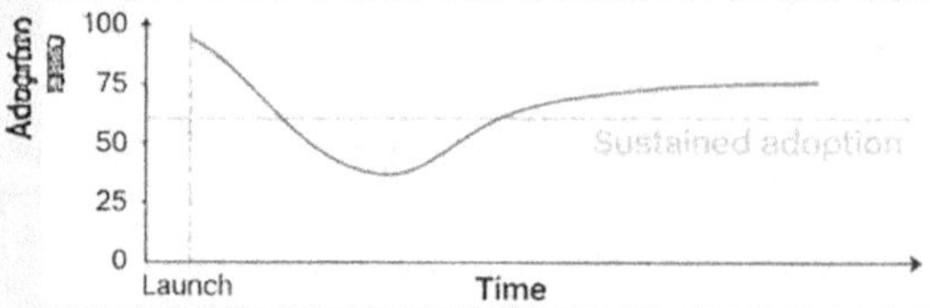

From Communicator to Workflow Architect

Shifting from Messages to Workflows

1. Change now lives inside workflows, not just comms plans.
2. AI is redesigning tasks and handoffs.
3. Change professionals shape how new work gets done.
4. Workflow architecture maps inputs, decisions, tools, handoffs.
5. Process-aware change leaders gain strategic influence.

What you Need to Remember

Go where the work happens

Map real processes, not org charts.
Change lives in how work flows.

Think like a workflow architect

Spot where AI can add value,
and where human judgment is essential.

Earn your seat at the table

Help leaders see new work clearly.
Clarity on humans and AI
builds trust and better outcomes.

Old change approach		New approach
announce & train	→	design the workflow
top-down instructions	→	workflow-based change
broadcast to everyone	→	targeted by role and handoff
hope for adoption	→	designed for outcomes

Good next moves

- Map one critical workflow.
- Mark AI steps vs human steps.
- Test it with frontline staff.

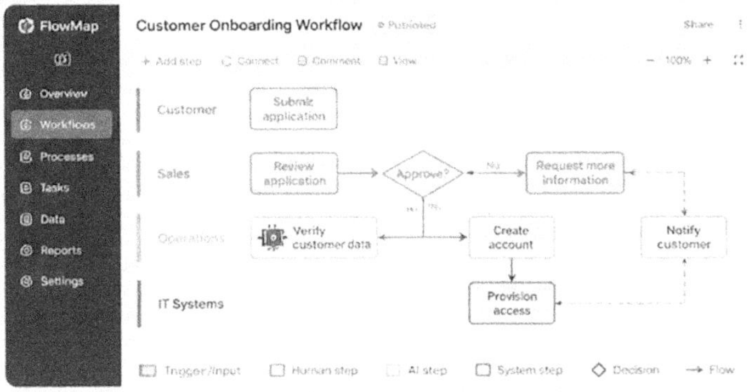

Designing Change Around Actual Work

Designing Change Around Real Tasks

1. **Start with the task, not the announcement.**
Understand what people are trying to get done before you change it.

2. **Map the new workflow with AI in the loop to reveal where humans are essential.**
Make AI's role visible so the right decisions stay with people.

3. **Fix workflow design, not "attitude", to remove friction.**
Improve steps, tools, and handoffs—people adapt when work gets easier.

4. **Change professionals act as workflow advocates for users.**
Bring user voice, challenge assumptions, and protect what helps people do their best work.

5. **Partner closely with IT, operations, and product.**
Great change happens when everyone builds it together, not in silos.

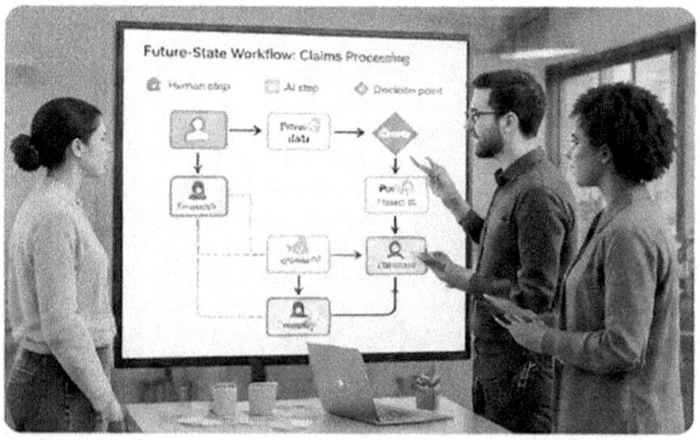

What you Need to Remember

Begin with the new task
Real understanding comes from the work people do, not the change message.

Design for human–AI handoffs
Make AI do the predictable and people do the judgement—at every decision point.

Show up as a workflow partner
Help teams remove friction, build confidence, and deliver better outcomes together.

1 Map current work → 2 Prototype new workflow → 3 Test with real users → 4 Tune with tech + ops

In practice, focus on:

- High-impact tasks
- Messy handoffs
- Hidden rework

Change Impact Dashboard

Process map (future state)

Tasks automated: 38%

Cycle time reduction: 25%

Friction reports: 12 Open, 3 new this week

Human step · AI step · Decision point

From Training Owner to Capability Strategist

Expanding the Role

1. **Beyond the training calendar.** Owning sessions and completions is only one slice of capability.
2. **Start with future skills.** Ask what people must be able to do to thrive with AI-enabled work.
3. **Build human + AI capability together.** Design learning so tools, skills, and judgement develop in tandem.
4. **Think across the system.** Connect learning design, role redesign, career paths, and performance expectations.
5. **Sit at the intersection.** Partner with HR, L&D, and transformation leaders as a single capability system.

What you Need to Remember

1. Aim: Design capability, not courses.

Focus on what people must be able to deliver, not just what they've attended.

2. Lens: Human + AI, role by role.

Map which tasks AI absorbs, how human judgement and collaboration create value, and where new habits are needed.

3. Outcome: Become a strategic partner.

Use capability insights to shape org design, change roadmaps, and measures of success.

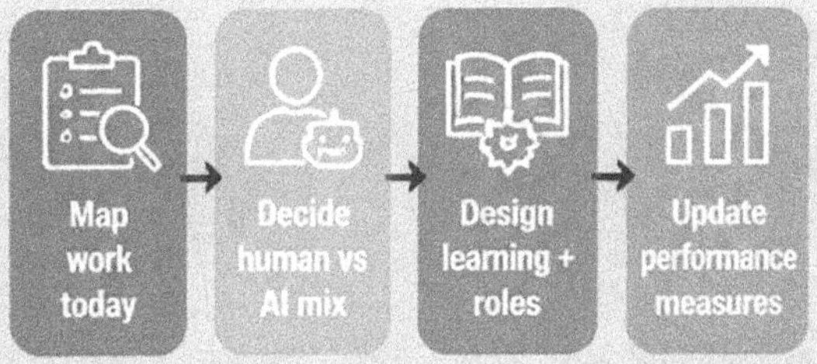

In every project, ask:

- What future capabilities are we building?
- How will humans and AI share the work?
- How will we know capability has improved?

Building Human and AI Capability Together

Designing Capability for Human + AI Teams

1. **Blend tool skills with thinking skills.**
   Teach prompting, analysis, and how to question results together.
2. **Spot AI literacy gaps.**
   Map who is confident, who is hesitant, and where work is at risk.
3. **Use peer learning and live work.**
   Short demos + side-by-side practice beat long classrooms.
4. **Refresh little and often.**
   Schedule capability 'sprints' as tools, policies, and risks change.
5. **Protect equity and judgment.**
   Make it safe to challenge AI and to slow down when stakes are high.

What you Need to Remember

Tools + Thinking, not either/or.

Every AI rollout must build critical thinking, communication, and judgment alongside feature training.

Practice in real work.

Give people safe sandboxes, peer support, and small experiments embedded in everyday tasks.

Learn → Try → Reflect

Keep the strategy alive.

Review capability quarterly: what changed, who is being left behind, and which new skills matter most?

Design Check

- Who needs which skills?
- Where will they practice?
- How will we support reflection?

Signals it's Working

- People ask better questions of AI.
- Colleagues share prompts and tips.
- Usage spreads beyond early adopters.

From Adoption Tracker to Value Partner

From activity reports to value stories

1. Completion is necessary, not the goal – trackers and surveys show activity, not impact.
2. Value partnership links behaviour change directly to measurable business results.
3. Shift the question: not 'Did they adopt it?' but 'Did it make a measurable difference?'
4. Talk the metrics: productivity, quality, cost, and risk become your core language.
5. Co-design with finance, operations, and data teams so 'better' is defined up-front.

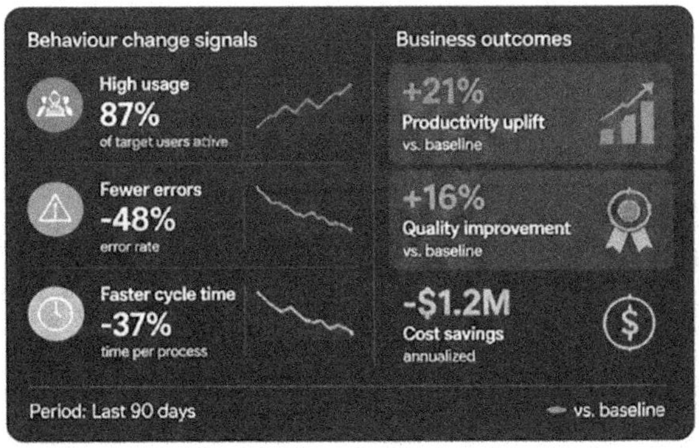

What you Need to Remember

Think like a value partner, not a reporter.

Use adoption data as a starting point, then ask what changed in the work and the numbers.

Define 'better' with the business before you launch.

Agree target shifts in productivity, quality, cost, or risk and how they'll be measured.

Tell impact stories backed by evidence.

Show the line from new behaviours to dashboards and decisions leaders care about.

Use this after every programme

- Map key behaviours you needed to change.
- Pair each behaviour with one or two hard metrics.
- Review results with finance / ops and refine the next wave.

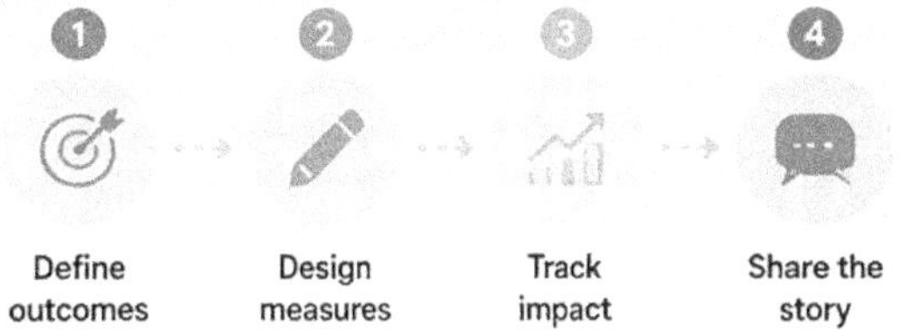

Connecting Behaviour Change to Measurable Outcomes

Design the Measurement Architecture

1 Define success before launch

Agree the business outcomes, target levels, and timeframe up front.
If you can't measure it, you can't improve it.

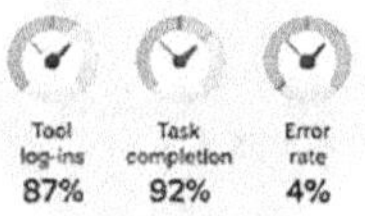

2 Choose leading indicators

Track early signals that show whether behaviours are changing and adoption is on track.
They predict future outcomes.

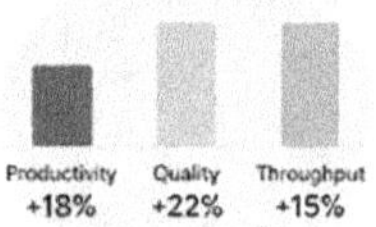

3 Track lagging outcomes

Measure the results that matter to the business after behaviours have had time to stick.
These prove the impact.

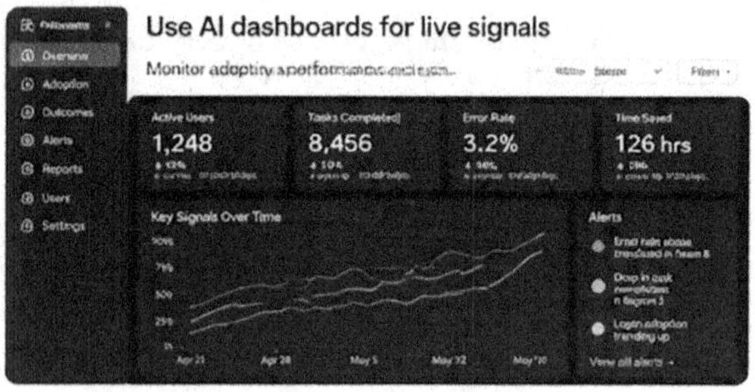

Use AI dashboards for live signals

5 Tell the value story

Turn data into insight. Combine numbers with human stories to show why the change matters and what comes next.

What you Need to Remember

Start with the end in mind

Define the outcomes you care about before anything goes live.
Clear outcomes drive better design, better signals, and better results.

Balance leading and lagging signals

Leading indicators show early movement.
Lagging outcomes prove impact.
Use both to guide decisions.

Combine data with human stories

Numbers build credibility.
Stories build understanding and action.
Together they drive lasting change.

From behaviour to outcomes

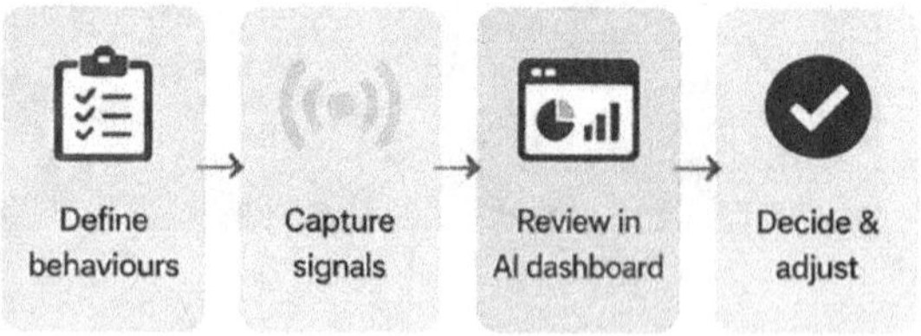

Before launch: agree the 3–5 metrics that matter most

During rollout: review adoption data weekly and act on red flags

When reporting up: pair every key metric with one real user story

Leading Continuous Transformation

Leading in a Constant-Change Environment

1. **AI cycles move in weeks, not years.**
   Treat AI changes as a rolling wave, not a one-off programme.
2. **There is no steady state.**
   Assume tools, roles, and processes will keep evolving.
3. **Build organisational resilience, not just one more plan.**
   Focus on how the whole system absorbs shocks and learns.
4. **Design the conditions for change.**
   Shape decision rights, information flow, and simple rules so adaptation is normal work.
5. **Invest in culture, leadership habits, and structural capacity.**
   Psychological safety, learning routines, and flexible structures beat rigid roadmaps.

What you Need to Remember

Think capacity, not projects.
Your job is to help the organisation get better at changing all the time, not to 'finish' change.

Hard-wire adaptive habits.
Coach leaders to run short learning cycles, talk openly about uncertainty, and reward experimentation.

Tune culture and structure together.
Pair psychological safety and clear purpose with rhythms, roles, and forums that make fast adjustment possible.

From Linear Change to Continuous Transformation

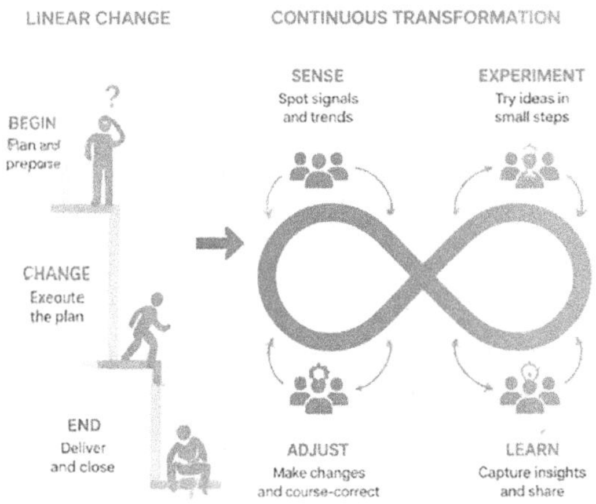

Leader moves this week:
- Shorten planning horizons.
- Add a standing 'learning from change' slot to team meetings.
- Ask: what capacity are we building, not just which change are we delivering?

Measure resilience:
speed of learning, quality of decisions, and how people feel under pressure.

Operating in a World Where Change Never Really Stops

Operating in Continuous Change

1. **Protect practitioner resilience**
   Manage energy, recovery, and boundaries to stay effective.
2. **Prioritise what truly needs a full response**
   Focus time and attention on what creates meaningful impact.
3. **Reuse lightweight change patterns**
   Use proven, simple patterns to move faster with less effort.
4. **Rely on community and peer support**
   Share, ask, and learn together to solve problems faster.
5. **Model adaptability yourself**
   Demonstrate curiosity, flexibility, and calm in uncertainty.

What you Need to Remember

Sustain the humans doing the work
Resilient, supported people are the real engine of change.

Don't turn every shift into a programme
Not every change needs a formal plan. Right-size the response.

Show up as the adaptability you're asking for
Your mindset and behaviour set the tone for the whole system.

1. **Sense change** — Scan the environment, listen to signals, and understand the impact. →
2. **Choose response** — Decide the right level of response and pick the best fit. →
3. **Apply pattern & learn** — Take action using a proven pattern and capture what we learn.

Reflect, adapt, and improve for next time

Footer: Use this in practice

- Schedule resilience check-ins for change teams
- Keep a small library of go-to change patterns
- Stay plugged into your peer community

More in the AI Visual Reference Series

This is the first title in a growing series, each volume applying the same visual, look-it-up approach to a different professional domain. New titles are added regularly. Search "AI Awareness Visual Reference" or visit www.aiawareness.ai for the complete, up-to-date list.

#	Title
1	AI Governance and Ethics Visual Reference
2	AI in Change Management Visual Reference
3	AI in Risk and Audit Visual Reference
4	AI in Cybersecurity Visual Reference
5	AI in Data Analytics Visual Reference
6	AI in Knowledge Management Visual Reference
7	AI in Research and Development Visual Reference
8	AI in Innovation and Digital Transformation Visual Reference
9	AI in Product Management Visual Reference
10	AI in IT Management Visual Reference
11	AI in Human Resources Visual Reference
12	AI in Learning and Development Visual Reference
13	AI in Executive Leadership Visual Reference
14	AI in Legal and Compliance Visual Reference
15	AI in Marketing Visual Reference
16	AI in Sales Visual Reference
17	AI in Customer Experience Visual Reference
18	AI in Customer Service Visual Reference
19	AI in Finance Visual Reference
20	AI in Sustainability and ESG Reporting Visual Reference
21	AI in Facility Management Visual Reference
22	AI in Supply Chain Management Visual Reference
23	AI in Procurement Visual Reference
24	AI in Project Management Visual Reference
25	AI in Operations Visual Reference
26	AI in Manufacturing Visual Reference

#	Title
27	AI in Construction and Engineering Visual Reference
28	AI in Real Estate Visual Reference
29	AI in Transportation and Logistics Visual Reference
30	AI in Energy and Utilities Visual Reference
31	AI in Telecommunications Visual Reference
32	AI in Agriculture and Food Production Visual Reference
33	AI in Financial Institutions Visual Reference
34	AI in Insurance Visual Reference
35	AI in Healthcare Visual Reference
36	AI in Pharmaceuticals and Life Sciences Visual Reference
37	AI in Public Sector and Government Visual Reference
38	AI in Retail Visual Reference
39	AI in Hospitality Visual Reference
40	AI in Media and Entertainment Visual Reference

www.ingramcontent.com/pod-product-compliance
Lightning Source LLC
LaVergne TN
LVHW060451061126
851857LV00016B/1791
* 9 7 9 8 9 0 1 4 8 9 2 3 9 *